SINCLAIR O'NEILL

Belinda Sinclair is a writer and radio producer. She has a particular interest in classic aviation, the Second World War and unusual stories about real people. She was born in Maidstone and now lives in Surrey.

Barbara O'Neill is a writer and broadcaster. Like all writers she is a hopeless procrastinator. This book is a miracle. Born in the New Forest, she lives in Sussex - by the sea.

Cutmill Books
Sinclair O'Neill
P O Box 143
Chichester PO18 8WD

First Edition 2002

Copyright © Sinclair O'Neill 2002

ISBN No: 0-9542952-0-X

Published by
Cutmill Books

Printed, bound and set in Comic Sans by
RPM Reprographics
Chichester, West Sussex PO19 2PR

Cover design by Eric North

Illustrations by Alan Teece

All rights reserved. No part of this publication may be reproduced, stored in a retrieval system, or transmitted in any form or by any means, electronic, mechanical, photocopying, recording or otherwise, without prior permission of the publishers.

This book is sold subject to the condition that it shall not, by way of trade or otherwise, be lent, re-sold, hired out or otherwise circulated without the publisher's prior consent in any form of binding or cover other than that in which it is published and without a similar condition including this condition being imposed on the subsequent purchaser.

WARTIME WOMEN

Memories of a Forties Generation

Sinclair O'Neill

Cutmill Books/Publishers

PREFACE

This book was conceived during a holiday in Hastings. While eating lunch at his great grandmother's house, his head filled with William the Conqueror, eye loss, chain mail and battle, the eight year old boy spied a badge fixed to her scarf.

'What's that badge, Granny?'
'It's the Royal Artillery Crest.'
'Why are you wearing it?'
'Because I was in the war.'
'The war? Did you have a bow and arrow?'
'No, dear, I'm not that old. My war was the Second World War and I had an anti-aircraft gun.'

For each of the stories in this book, there are many more that remain untold. Some women did not live to tell of their experiences, others declined to do so. Some never had the opportunity. Whatever the reason, one outstanding fact remains; whatever they did, however small, however seemingly insignificant, everybody who did something, 'did their bit', and paved the way for our lives today.

With special thanks to Felicity Newton

INTRODUCTION

by
The Right Honourable Baroness Boothroyd of Sandwell PC

Anybody who lived during the Second World War lived through a time of great awakening. For the first time, the world came to Great Britain. This war was not merely a far away foreign conflict; it was home war, fought as much on our soil as abroad.

Despite the tragedy and the trauma, those six years were a time of great excitement, an era of new opportunity and a challenge to old ways.

Suddenly, en masse, women had a presence. No longer inaudible participants, they came to the fore and filled the void left by the men who had gone to fight. They went into the factories and onto the land, behind enemy lines, into the skies and into the armed services. They worked the transport network, the defence systems, the fire and ambulance brigades and joined the Home Guard. And when they had finished their day, they went home and did their own 'women's work'.

Like the men, these women gave half a decade of their life to the country. Yet, unlike them, they were never really recognised; never really thanked or acknowledged for what they did.

While the country gradually recovered, their efforts were overlooked and they slipped back into the support framework of everyday life.

The women of the Second World War are now old; some are no longer with us. But what they achieved all those years ago is the basis of our life today. Had they not 'done their bit,' then how much of what we now take for granted, would be there?

FOREWORD
by Dame Vera Lynn

Whilst it is right that the men who fought in the Second World War are commemorated each year, the efforts of the thousands of women who kept the country going in their absence has never been fully recognised.

These were the women who became pilots and flight engineers, joined the Land Army and fed the country, managed the forests, drove ambulances, worked in factories, in radar, on gun sites, built aircraft, made ammunition and became skilled engineers. Yet the same women also did what women were supposed to do - feed and raise the children, queue for rations and clear up the debris after the bombing.

This generation neither questioned nor balked at what they were expected to do. They just got on with it - and made it all work. No-one said it better than Bacon: 'Prosperity doth best discover vice, but adversity doth best discover virtue.'

After the war finished, they slipped back into peacetime, into a world that was changed forever. A world that despite their public wartime presence, forgot to thank them.

CONTENTS

Preface
Introduction   The Rt Hon Baroness Boothroyd
Foreword   Dame Vera Lynn

AIR TRANSPORT AUXILIARY
Chapter 1   Lettice Curtis   13
Chapter 2   Jackie Sorour   19
Chapter 3   Diana Barnato   29

LAND ARMY AND TIMBER CORPS   38
Chapter 4   Daisy Lodge   41
Chapter 5   Margaret Bellingham   45
Chapter 6   Barbara Dunlop   48
Chapter 7   Barbara Hooper   53
Chapter 8   Cecilia Rockliffe   56
Chapter 9   Kay O'Neill   60

THE CHILDREN   65
Chapter 10   Betty Waters   66
Chapter 11   Marion Wormull   72
Chapter 12   Pamela Briant   82
Chapter 13   Doris Russell   86
Chapter 14   Elsie Burberry   91

THE ARMED SERVICES   95
Chapter 15   Isabel Eakins   96
Chapter 16   Muriel Poole   107
Chapter 17   Peggy Steel   113
Chapter 18   Mildred Veal   116
Chapter 19   Jane Pope   122
Chapter 20   Pat Beveridge   129
Chapter 21   Joyce Tapsell   136
Chapter 22   Anthea Gregson   142
Chapter 23   Shirley Pettyfer   147

Chapter 24	Betty Kerr	152
Chapter 25	Joy Schooley	157
Chpater 26	Anne McHugh	163
Chapter 27	Vera Wilson	168
Chapter 28	Olive Walker	175
Chapter 29	Doreen Lloyd	182
CIVIL DEFENCE		190
Chapter 30	Joan Crump	192
WOMEN'S VOLUNTARY SERVICE		196
Chapter 31	Irene Parnell	198
AIR RAID PRECAUTIONS		204
Chapter 32	Winnie Viner	206
Chapter 33	Molly Hutchins	209
Chapter 34	Nancy Denman	213
Chapter 35	Margaret Cornish	217
Chapter 36	Margaret McFarlane	225
Chapter 37	Audrey Boyd	235
Chapter 38	Vera Manley	239
Chapter 39	Pauline Smith	243
Chapter 40	Lily Wray	247

Acknowledgements by kind permission of:
The Croydon Advertiser Group
Aeroplane Monthly
Times Newspapers

Whilst every effort has been made to ensure factual accuracy, Sinclair O'Neill apologise for any errors.

THE AIR TRANSPORT AUXILIARY

Twenty years after their appearance in the Great War, aircraft were at the forefront of a new conflict. Recognising their potential as a means of communication, a plan to use civilian pilots, including experienced women, was drawn up in early 1939.

As the fighting escalated, so did the original plan. Now more than just a means of communication, and with able-bodied civilian pilots joining the armed services, a new organisation was formed to ferry aircraft around the country.

The Air Transport Auxiliary (ATA) delivered machines from factories to storage, and to airfields. Staffed by men ineligible for active service, in 1940, the ATA recruited eight women pilots.

Initially entrusted with moving older training craft to safe sites, the eight women were gradually allowed to fly other machines. More women joined them, until there were over one hundred and fifty female pilots flying every type of allied aircraft.

By the end of the war, the ATA had delivered 3,911 aeroplanes. With a ground crew of over 3,000, the ATA established an impressive safety record. Unfortunately, some pilots were lost, Amy Johnson amongst them.

CHAPTER ONE

Lettice Curtis - Pilot

For six years, the ATA kept the RAF supplied with aircraft. By the end of the war, they had accrued an incredible number of flying hours and were amongst some of the most experienced pilots in the world. They had also established an enviable safety record.

Barnstorming, or joy riding as it was known, was a popular attraction at fairs and events across the country during the 1920s and 30s. It had started as a way for redundant First World War pilots to earn a living in peacetime, and had developed as more people took to the skies. It was while leaning over the fence at her local airfield in Denbury near Torquay, Devon, that Lettice Curtis first considered learning to fly.

'I remember it quite clearly. I was watching a plane coming in to land. In those days there was nothing set up; it was just a field and I remember the pilot walking over and asking me something. There was nobody else to ask.'

After she had answered his question, she posed one of her own:

'Can women fly?'

On hearing that they could, she made up her mind.

'I decided there and then to be a pilot; I can still

remember that conversation to this day.'

In 1938, on gaining her commercial licence, she got a job with an air survey company. Two days before war was declared, she was ordered to fly her aircraft to Weston super Mare, as it had been requisitioned by the Air Ministry. After more than a year of flying professionally, she was tired of earning her living as a pilot.

'I'd done a lot of flying for the gun aimers before the war and it was all rather boring. You flew back and forth along a route for hours on end so that anti-aircraft gun crews could aim their guns at you and practise for the real thing. It was all rather tedious but the money was good. You got something like a pound an hour, which was a lot then.'

Pauline Gower was an experienced pilot and navigator, tasked by the Air Ministry to manage the introduction of women pilots. Although she did not fly with the ATA, she was determined that women should prove their ability, despite public contempt:

'The menace is the woman who thinks that she ought to be flying a high speed bomber when she really has not the intelligence to scrub the floor of a hospital properly, or who wants to nose around as an air raid warden and yet can't cook her husband's dinner'. - C.C.Grey, editor of The Aeroplane.

She had already recruited eight women by the time she approached Lettice.

'Our names were on the register of qualified pilots but I turned them down first time. I was rather disenchanted with the whole flying thing. But then Pauline Gower wrote to me again and I thought I'd better do my bit, so I joined up. That was in June 1940.'

Lettice Curtis was posted to Hatfield in Hertfordshire, to an all-female ferry pool. Men were based in nearby White Waltham.

'We had to clear Tiger Moths at first. We took them up to Scotland, to Lossiemouth and Kinloss for storage. It was to save the chaps the indignity of having to do it. Tiger Moths were only trainers.'

The women pilots were not permitted to fly operational aircraft in the early days of the war but, as it dragged on, the rules changed. By 1941, they were allowed to ferry obsolete aircraft such as Lysanders. According to Lettice, the women pilots pushed themselves to cope with things for which they were ill-prepared, for fear of letting the side down.

'In the summer of 1941, I was sent to be checked out on Masters and Oxfords. I'd had a commercial licence for several years by then, but it was on civilian aircraft, not military. We had just five hours practice on these aircraft - and were then passed to fly anything that we were told to. It's a wonder we didn't kill ourselves. But we didn't say anything in case the licences were taken away from us.'

The men were in no better position, although their lack of experience did not seem to warrant the same attention.

'I remember once bouncing a Lysander - a minor bounce, but there was such a terrible fuss. It was apparently proof that we women were not to be trusted. If a man had done it - which they frequently did - nothing would have been said. It wouldn't even have been noticed.'

Later in the war, a school was set up to give ATA pilots some familiarisation training but for those who joined early on, it really was just a question of getting in, being talked through the controls, and taking off.

Then in September 1941, the ban on women flying fighters was lifted. Lettice flew one almost immediately.

'I was stuck in Scotland and had to phone the operations manager to see if there was anything for me to take south so that I could get home. When you delivered planes, you had to find your own way back, so we used to try and find aircraft that needed to be delivered somewhere near to home. He gave me a Hurricane - I told him I wasn't cleared but he said women were OK now and that was it. I got in, he ran through the controls, I took off and that was that. I just had to work it out as I went along. I was more scared of letting the women down than crashing.'

Later, when the Hamble Ferry Pool was turned into an all women flying base, Lettice was sent there.

'By that time, we were so experienced and the need was so great, that we were allowed to fly anything. About a month after I was posted there, I was sent back to White Waltham to be checked out on bombers. I was given a Blenheim and off I went, cleared for all two-engined bombers. I think I got a chit for a Wellington next. It was quite incredible - just like that!'

Although she recognised the ability of her colleagues, Lettice was keen to learn from the experienced male pilots. Eventually, she transferred to Number One Ferry Pool at White Waltham, to work with them.

'I just felt I could learn so much from them and I had a super time there.'

Shortly after, she went on a Halifax course and was cleared to fly all four-engined heavy bombers, including one of the specially adapted aircraft flown by 617 Squadron to bomb the Ruhr Valley Dams - the Dam Buster Raid.

'I was the first one (woman) to be cleared on the big bombers and to fly a Lancaster. These were huge planes and were designed for a crew. But like all flying, we were on our own. Nobody to help us, nobody to check queries with. It would have been quite daunting if we'd started to think about it I suppose.'

After six years of war, the end came very quickly for the ATA pilots.

'We got a note round that just said, "We're closing", and that was that. I remember thinking that I'd have to find a job - and I had to move out of my billet and find a place to live.'

Despite her substantial flying experience, and her proven ability, the pre-war prejudice returned almost immediately.

'I was a pilot. I'd earned my living as one for nearly a decade and had flown most types of aircraft. But the emerging airlines wouldn't even look at us women. Occasionally you got an interview, but we knew it was just an opportunity for them to see what you looked like.'

Eventually, Lettice got a job as operations manager for the Civil Aviation Authority - the first woman ever to do so. But even then, discrimination was rife.

'The Director was horrified at having a woman in his directorate and he tried to use me as his PA, but he finally got the message.'

Her job was to plan the conversion and installation of aviation services for the civilian airfields that had been under RAF control. It included establishing air traffic control and meteorological facilities.

Later, she got a job as a test pilot at Boscombe Down, checking civilian aircraft for airworthiness, and testing aircraft involved in accidents, to establish the cause of the crash.

'I was accepted on merit, but then the men kicked up a fuss about having a woman working amongst them on an equal footing. They refused to let me take up the pilot job, but they did allow me to join the performance team on the flights, writing reports and collecting data.'

It seems that whilst they were willing to let her risk her life along with them in an aircraft not yet airworthy, or one known to be faulty, the men were not willing to allow her any control over her own destiny.

Lettice Curtis later became a flight developer for the Fairey Aviation Company and was one of the engineering team responsible for setting up the West Drayton Air Traffic Control Centre in West London. She now lives in Berkshire and is still involved with aviation. She gained her helicopter licence in 1990.

CHAPTER TWO

Jackie Sorour - Pilot

Even as a young girl growing up in South Africa, Jackie Sorour wanted to fly. Yet quite why she decided on that particular occupation is unclear, especially as she readily admits, she was scared of everything and anything.

'My grandmother brought me up and she wouldn't let me do anything in case I hurt myself. I was scared of everything and quite the wrong person to take up flying. I am naturally a coward and I suppose I took on her feeling of apprehension and it turned into fear.'

When she was seven, she saw something in the sky that she was sure was a sign she would spend her life among the clouds. She remembers being enthralled by the sight.

'I know it sounds incredible but I saw it clearly. I had just started school in the mountains and we used to get very violent thunderstorms up there. I remember watching, fascinated, as the cloud cleared, leaving just a few beautiful cumuli clouds.'

As her attention was attracted by the noise of an aeroplane, she looked towards it and believed she saw an angel.

'There was this figure flying quite clearly above the plane. Its hands were as if in prayer and it was robed. It stayed with the biplane until it went into the next bit of cloud. It seemed absolutely real.'

That experience marked the start of her life in aviation, despite her belief that she was a coward. However, feelings of apprehension did little to deter her, even when she became the first South African woman to make a parachute jump. She broke her leg in the process.

Still only in her mid-teens, she left for England, her leg still in plaster from the parachute incident, intent on enrolling at aeronautical college. She was determined to be a professional pilot and the place to do that was at Oxford, using Witney aerodrome.

After little more than a year at the college, war broke out.

'Our exams were due to start on November 19th, 1939, but the war started in September. So that was that. None of us got to take them although we had all studied and learned the thirteen subjects required to be a professional pilot.'

In August, the trainee pilots at the college were called up to form a civil air guard. By then, she had clocked up over four hundred hours flying time, far more than many enlisted pilots. Yet, in the confusion of those early years of the war, she was turned away from flying jobs.

'I was seventeen but I looked about twelve - I just didn't look the part. So they told me to go away. This happened three times and they just wouldn't believe me.'

A solution was quickly found. She was diverted from flying duties and seconded to other work.

'They put me onto direction finding radio - it was what we had before we had Radar, and it was all because they thought I looked too young. They wanted pilots to look about twenty-five and I didn't, so I had to do that instead.'

Between November 1939 and July 1941, Jackie Sorour worked in Radar until finally she was released to become a pilot. But even then, the transfer did not go smoothly.

'Pauline Gower called me down to Hatfield and tested me. I had to do three landings there and I did each of them perfectly, but they still didn't want me to fly. I had to produce my birth certificate and, even Pauline Gower, who was a pilot herself and who knew what a good pilot I was, tried to insist that I stayed in Radar. It was only when the sergeant persuaded her that I was more valuable flying, that she gave in. After all, it took about six weeks to train a Radar officer, but I had already got hours of experience in the air and had been flying for years already - even though I was always scared!'

She became the fifteenth woman pilot to join the ATA, one after Lettice Curtis. However, even by then and with Pauline Gower on her side, Jackie still had difficulties with her age.

'I had this argument everytime. Eventually, Pauline added a couple of years to my documents so that I was then twenty instead of eighteen. The Air Ministry were very hot about insurance and I was old enough, but the age increase seemed to do the trick; I was posted within three weeks.'

She was sent to the all woman ferry pool at Hatfield where the de Havilland brothers built Mosquito aircraft. She was based there for a year.

With pilots scattered at different airfields, an air-taxi

system was introduced to take them back to the pool. The legendary Amy Johnson was one of the taxi pilots as well as a ferry pilot, and Jackie recalled how, one day, Amy turned up to take her back home.

'I'd delivered a plane to Llandaw near Cardiff in Wales and I had to get back to Hamble where I was based. Thick fog came down and we were stuck - we couldn't take off so we had to stay put.'

Although Wales is not far in air miles from Hamble, flight paths were crucial because of the barrage balloon lines around cities and dock areas. ATA pilots were forbidden to fly above cloud. Although Jackie was fully trained and had studied meteorology, even she was not allowed to fly anything other than contact - within sight of the ground.

'We made the most of our time in the city - we went shopping. We had so little time off normally that this was a real treat anyway, but for me it was really special as there I was - just eighteen and walking around with *the* Amy Johnson. She was in her late thirties then and she was wonderful, very sweet, and I was so proud because people were looking and nudging each other and saying, "That's Amy Johnson." She was so well known.'

Jackie and Amy spent two days in Cardiff. They went to the cinema, Amy bought her sister some shoes, and gave Jackie some chocolate. Just one week later, on January 5th 1941, Amy Johnson was killed, ferrying an Airspeed Oxford to Kidlington.

Jackie, Amy and another woman, had each been told to transfer an Oxford to the aerodrome. Amy was bringing hers from Blackpool and Jackie remembers they had been told they had to get the aircraft there at all costs. The weather was severe.

'It was a terrible day, lots of mist and cloud and drizzle. I had put my undercarriage and flaps down so that I could fly closer to the ground and try to see where I was going. But at very low altitude, you seem to be flying faster than you really are and so you have to react more quickly, and I was very conscious that these aircraft had to be delivered.'

As the three pilots made their way to Kidlington, the weather deteriorated. Jackie and the other pilot descended to a hundred and fifty feet but, Amy Johnson, coming from Blackpool, took longer, by which time thick fog had settled. Jackie maintains she became disorientated by a combination of factors.

'She had to go over the top and there's always a westerly wind that blows across Britain. It was strong that day higher up and, with the cloud, I think she was blown off course. She couldn't see the ground to find her way and had to descend through it. Unfortunately, she came down in the water and was never found. It was terribly sad. She was such a good navigator and so experienced.'

Jackie also believes that their lack of training had some part in the loss of ATA pilots. They had to learn the different quirks of each aircraft on the job, and sometimes that meant mastering up to five different machines in one day.

'We just got in and if you were lucky you might get a couple of circuits. But usually we just had some notes that we read when we got in and that was it. Some people, unfortunately, got it wrong.'

Later on, training was given, but that was no help to the early ATA pilots. They did not fly on instruments and, according to Jackie, they were not taught to release their parachutes either - although they carried them.

'It was probably because we weren't supposed to jump out of the aircraft before we'd delivered it!'

ATA pilots generally flew short routes, mostly confined to British airspace, although they did ferry overseas in the latter part of the war. They usually flew alone except where another crew member was needed to assist in flight operations. This meant the Air Ministry could save a full crew, risking fewer lives, and expending less engine power.

'They were just starting to introduce women flight engineers. On some bombers you took off on just two engines and once you were airborne, the flight engineer would switch to the other two, then switch back for landing. The aircraft was much lighter because it had no bombs on board.'

Sadly, the Air Ministry's fears came true on one particular day. Jackie was flying in formation with one other aircraft, crewed by a woman pilot and a woman flight engineer. The two aircraft became separated when they hit bad weather.

'We were flying to Lasham near Odiham when we came across snow and thunder. I had been trained on meteorology at college so I was lucky but not many of the others had. I flew around it but I think they went through it.'

Jackie followed the other aircraft in to Lasham. As she landed, she noticed a big black patch on the runway.

'They'd exploded on landing. I don't know exactly what happened but it was snowing and thundery and maybe they came in too fast at too low an altitude. If the pilot had pulled the stick back too far she may have stalled, but they were both dead. The pilot was Dora Lang but I never knew the flight engineer's name. But I do remember that she was one of the first and I can see her now - she was twenty-one, and very sweet, very pretty. The burnt black patch was all that was left of them.'

The continual question of Jackie's age arose periodically throughout her ATA days. Even mid-way through the war, a flight sergeant tried to stop her flying.

'He thought I was some nutty schoolgirl trying to take a plane and he wouldn't believe me when I said who I was. That was another round of phone calls and lots of checking up before I was allowed to do my job.'

On another occasion, she was at the controls of an Anson air-taxi when one of the engines failed. It was not unusual, and it was something that she had experienced before. However, this time she was nervous.

'Well, I had thirteen ATA pilots and parachutes on board and we lost an engine; it just cut out and it was a twin-engine aircraft. One of the older women was sitting up front with skinny old me and I was at the controls. I could see her looking at me and watching me; it was clear they were all wondering whether I would manage to land us safely. Well, of course I could, I knew that, and I would have been fine on my own. But with all of them watching me and waiting for me to make a mistake, I was really nervous. But we landed perfectly well, and they changed their attitude after that, once they'd seen what I could do.'

Her training saved her more than once.

'I lost an engine in a Beaufighter - that's a medium range American bomber but that was OK and I just went into the nearest airfield. It had also happened in a Hudson - another American plane, and they had electric everything. If the engine failed so did the electricity.'

This is where her experience as a pilot really showed through. Given that ATA pilots delivered anything, anywhere, Jackie was frequently called upon to make difficult landings.

'The American planes were usually big and if we landed them at a large airfield, that was no problem. But often it was tight, and we had to get it spot on or else crash.'

She soon established a name for herself as a pilot who delivered on time with the plane intact, and was almost an Air Ministry mascot. However, she maintains the reason she persevered was quite simple.

'Once I'd taken off, I carried on to where I was going because I was too scared to turn round and go back, especially if I'd already come through bad weather. So I just kept going - and prayed very hard. By the end of the war, I'd ferried 1,499 aircraft.'

When the fighting finished, Jackie was one of six women ferry pilots to be seconded to the RAF Volunteer Reserve (RAFVR) and win their Air Force wings. She also applied to fly through the sound barrier, but discovered later on that her application had fallen foul of a particular male ego.

'There were several of us who wanted to, but I never heard any more, until I was at a dance with my husband in

1947. I danced with a particularly odious adjutant who had no idea of who I was or what I'd done. While we were dancing he discovered that I had been in the ATA and asked me if I knew "that awful Jackie Moggridge." I'd changed my name when I'd got married, of course. Well, I didn't answer, and he went on to tell me that, "she applied to fly through the sound barrier - who did she think she was?" He added that he had binned the form. At least I now knew why I had heard nothing!'

However, she unwittingly had the last laugh. When she returned to their table, her husband asked her to dance, Afterwards, they noticed that the adjutant and his wife were missing, and another one of their party looked perplexed.

'He said, "I think I've said the wrong thing. When I asked him (the adjutant) whether Jackie Moggridge was as good a dancer as she was a pilot, he asked me what I meant. When I said Jackie Moggridge - the woman you've just been dancing with - he went very pale and said they had an appointment, and left." The adjutant hadn't even had his dinner - and I hope he felt guilty for ever more!'

Jackie subsequently spent much of her working life as a commercial airline captain and became the first woman to attain that rank. However, even in civilian life and after her wartime experiences, she finally became disillusioned by the prejudice and narrow-minded behaviour that she frequently encountered.

'The final straw was when they gave captains four gold bands on their sleeves instead of three, and first officers three instead of two. I was taken aside and told that I could still only have three, although I was their most experienced and reliable captain. Apparently, the men wouldn't like it. Well, that was it - I hadn't really cared that much when they'd passed me off to passengers as the chief stewardess instead of the captain - I only wanted to fly - but when they did that, I'd had enough. They didn't like the fact that I looked just like a housewife at the controls. So, I did something that none of them could ever do - I went off and had babies!'

Jackie now lives in Somerset.

CHAPTER THREE

Diana Barnato - Pilot

'I still marvel at the saga that was the ATA - we had a conjurer, millionaires, all sorts, and they moulded us into something that could fly an aircraft - and safely.'

Diana Barnato joined the Air Transport Auxiliary in 1942. Being from a privileged background, she could probably have avoided war work altogether had she wanted to. She certainly could have avoided work that was dangerous. But the opportunity was too exciting to miss.

'I just wanted to fly. I learned just before the war. Imagine being given all those lovely aircraft - all sorts and completely free!'

Diana enlisted three years into the war. By then, a school to train ATA pilots had been set up at White Waltham near Reading.

'In my day, you did thirty cross-country flights in a Manchester. That was an open monoplane and it was so that you could learn the country below. It was also to learn where the barrage balloons were. It wasn't a good idea to fly into them.'

Barrage balloons were sited in various locations near

towns. According to Diana, they were a morale booster more than anything - but a pilot's nightmare.

'I think they got more of ours (planes) than theirs but they did stop the enemy from strafing ground installations. But they were a real hazard; you couldn't fly into them and get away with it - only one or two lucky ones managed that.'

Life was hectic. She worked six days a week, with just one rest day. The pressure of work, plus the fear of putting female pilots in a poor light, provided a distraction that did not afford her the luxury of being scared or worried about her own mortality.

'We flew in all weathers and although we'd been given basic training at White Waltham School, we were still ill-prepared. We weren't taught to fly in cloud or on instruments. That wasn't so much of a problem for the people who had flown before the war as they knew how to do this, but I didn't. I knew what the instruments were but had no idea how to use them. Looking back, I think that was very wrong and it's only by luck I survived. I did so many silly things because I didn't know any better.'

ATA pilots were supposed to navigate using an ordinary road map. To do this effectively, they had to stay beneath the cloud base. This plan was peppered with flaws.

'The basic premise was sound, I suppose. The danger was, if you went above the clouds you might run out of England, or not be able to get down through the cloud at your destination, or you'd get through the cloud and fly into a hill or something. Then you'd be no more but, more importantly, the aircraft would be broken. But you often ended up in cloud because the weather closed in. There was nothing you could do about that.'

On one particular occasion, had she obeyed instructions, Diana would not have survived. However, a combination of good fortune, chance and naivety saved the day.

'I'd gone out with Max Aitken - Lord Beaverbrook's son - and some of 601 Squadron one night. They were horrified to learn that I'd never been taught to fly on instruments and had no idea how to deal with cloud. So Max took his fountain pen out and drew an instrument panel on this beautiful pink linen tablecloth and they gave me a lesson on what to do.'

The timing could not have been better.

'The very next morning I was called straight out and had no time to change from my very smart, but very tight, fitted uniform skirt into trousers or a boiler suit. I was given a Spit and sent off over the Cotswolds. It was a lovely day, sunny and bright but suddenly, at 1,150 feet, I was in cloud. I went round and round but knew that I couldn't jump out because I had a skirt on and my parachute webbing meant that my panties and stockings would be exposed to the world. My only option was to try and do what Max had taught me the day before.'

Lost in cloud and fearing the exposure of what might be termed the indecency of her underwear - made from parachute silk - Diana acted out the lesson from the previous night. She had a fairly good idea of her location and a rough idea of her height from the ground, but that was all.

'I turned my reciprocal like Max had said, watched the altimeter and did all of that. The cloud was very thick and I couldn't see anything. But I knew that I had to get on with it. I decided I would break off at fifty feet, in retrospect, a barmy idea but I knew no different. At six hundred feet I thought I really must bale out but I just couldn't bring myself to do it. Then suddenly, I broke clear - I was at tree top level - literally tree top level.'

But Diana was not where she thought she was; she was six miles off target. Ironically, had she been accurate, she would have flown into the ground. Her actual landing place was at a lower altitude - and this saved her.

By a quirky coincidence, she had landed at RAF Windrush - the blind flying training centre. As she got out of her aircraft, an RAF sergeant approached her and said, 'I say Miss, you must be good on instruments!'

The incident frightened her but, again, it mattered a great deal not to let the side down.

'As I got out, my knees collapsed - I expect it was pure reaction, but I couldn't let him see, so I leaned in and pretended to do something in the cockpit. I just couldn't bear to let him see I was scared. But I was.'

Another reason for flying 'contact' was so ground troops could identify friendly aircraft, and deal with any enemy aircraft that were following them from above.

'The Bristol Channel was always a bit tricky, especially going from England to Wales. We used to clear from Cardiff and often you'd get puffs of smoke coming up from the ack-ack guns. The aircraft would rock about but I always managed to get through OK. I remember once seeing a notice at one of the pools. It said, "Any pilot who thinks they've been shot at by friendly guns, report to the commandant". I remember there was a huge queue!'

On one occasion the fire was not so friendly. This time,

it came from a lone German raider over Reading. Diana was a passenger in an Anson, piloted by Jim Mollison, Amy Johnson's ex-husband. The Anson was renowned for its lumbering slowness. There were puffs of smoke coming up through the cloud and Diana assumed it was the friendly ground troops at work again, or trains from the goods yards not far below.

'We were in low cloud, just chugging along and suddenly an aircraft was coming towards us. I was sitting next to Jim and assumed it was a plane flying on instruments and he hadn't noticed us. Jim yanked us sideways and as he did so, we saw the swastikas. I remember him saying: "It's a bloody Jerry!" and then yanking us back into the cloud as quick as he could. And do you know, he shot at us as he went by?'

The lone raider was a 'hit-and-run' plane. The strategy was to sneak over from Germany using bad weather as cover, drop a few small bombs and then go home. This one had already made his drop - the smoke Diana had seen - and was going round again before heading home.

'I had a guardian angel, I really did. That Anson was so slow that Jerry missed us. Mind you, when we landed and looked over the plane for holes, I was quite disappointed really!'

The ride in the Anson on that day was one of the few occasions when Diana had company in the skies. Most of the time she was alone.

'We flew by ourselves unless you couldn't work the emergency hatches from the pilot seat, or the design was such that you couldn't work the petrol single-handed. We took a stooge on the big planes - usually a flight engineer.

Or sometimes we had an air cadet - boys of fourteen upward. They'd been trained what to do if it went wrong, but that was it. Most of the time you were alone - we couldn't spare two pilots for one flight.'

Of all the aeroplanes she flew, Diana is sure of her favourite and least favourite.

'The Spitfire was beautiful - it was part of you and it was wonderful. Even the later ones with the heavier, longer Griffin engines were a pleasure to fly.'

At the other end of the spectrum, an amphibious biplane was a chore.

'I hated the Walrus - it was a Fleet Air Arm Air Sea Rescue thing and it was more like a boat than a plane. It was very slow and the controls had a mind of their own. You had to climb in through the tail or clamber up the side - you always broke your fingernails or bashed your elbows. And to get the thing in the air, you had to pull on the stick and it would bash you in the chest or the tummy. I hated them. We cleared loads of them from Cowes on the Isle of Wight. And the Sea Otter was dreadful, too. They staggered into the sky rather than took off. Dreadful.'

As the war in Europe came to an end, Diana flew planes to the Low Countries, Poland, Czechoslovakia and Germany. These forays abroad had an added attraction: shopping. Europeans were beginning to emerge from the long years of conflict.

'Their war was over, but we were still fighting. They had things like sugar, sweets and leather goods that we couldn't get in England. But for some reason, we had cocoa powder - they didn't - and cocoa powder wasn't rationed. So we used to take a supply of it with us and sell it. We then spent the money in Brussels or Bruges or wherever we were trying to get back from.'

There was one problem, however; in a small fighter plane room was limited. But years of experience had taught Diana to be inventive.

'In a fighter, your parachute fitted into a bucket compartment under the pilot's seat. A parachute sack could hold forty tins of cocoa, so it was a very useful thing. I always kept an empty one handy in case I got a trip abroad. I remember one man telling me how stupid I was - not because I'd die if I had to bale out but because I would reach my terminal velocity before the tins of cocoa did. We lived with death every day, so I suppose we'd got used to it.'

With the fighting in Europe over, the war in Japan staggered on. It was during those final months that Diana very nearly lost her life.

Typhoon fighters had a very powerful radial engine, and an unusual fixing under the propeller. Aware that this aircraft had been involved in twenty-six unexplained crashes, killing all twenty-six pilots, Diana took off for Kemble one day. As she flew north over the Swindon railway, she noticed a draught in the cockpit, despite it being closed in. It did not seem important, so she pulled her goggles down and thought nothing more of it. Once again, her guardian angel was watching over her.

'Suddenly, there was a big bang and there was metal everywhere, all around my face. I thought the engine had blown up; so I put the nose down to prevent a stall. As I did so, I realised I could see right through the floor of the plane. I could see control wires and then sky.'

The under carriage had blown away and Diana knew that the increased airflow would raise the stalling speed dramatically. Unless she could exceed it she would, literally, fall out of the sky. Again, luck was with her. Sure of her position, she opened the throttle fully and headed for the nearest airfield. As she circuited to land, she waggled the wings to attract attention, but nobody came out. Because of the speed, she could not use the flaps. Had she tried to do so, they would have ripped off and made the aircraft even more unstable - probably fatally. There was only one option left; to land at high speed and hope for the best.

   By some miracle she made it. As she taxied to the airfield hut she was met by a man she knew only as Ned, 'Ned in the Shed' as the pilots called him. He appeared totally unconcerned as he looked first at the Typhoon, and then at her.

   'Why have you brought us only half an aircraft, Miss Barnato?' he asked calmly.

   Diana's was the twenty-seventh Typhoon accident. Her survival meant that she was able to describe the sequence of events.

   'They thought it was tail flutter and thought they'd fixed it, but I wasn't so sure. Why had the undercarriage gone if it had been tail flutter?'

   The Typhoon problem became superfluous as the Asian war ended, but years later, she discovered the probable cause of her last minute dance with death.

   'I told this story on the radio and I got a letter from a woman who'd been a WAAF. She told me that it had been her Typhoon, and she was the flight engineer who'd fixed it. This woman was very small and had trouble reaching the fixing under the propeller shaft. Her supervisor had told her to leave it, assuring her that it would be all right. So she did.'

It seems that the loose fitting had worked even looser with constant flights and bumpy landings. Airflow through the consequent gaps had exerted pressure on the inside of the fuselage, eventually to the point where it blew out, ripping off the undercarriage in the process.

'I think what must have happened was that the undercarriage took away not only the floor but the rudder and the control wires. Those pilots had no way of controlling their aircraft and they crashed. But that didn't happen to me and I was all right.'

She was pleased to be reassured after all those years.

'It was nice to find out what had happened - and I suppose to know it wasn't something that I'd done. And the WAAF did say she was sorry!'

After the war, Diana obtained a commercial pilot's licence and became Corps Pilot for the Women's Junior Air Corps. She now lives in Surrey.

THE WOMEN'S LAND ARMY

The Women's Land Army originated during the First World War as a means of feeding the Nation. Just over twenty years later, it was resurrected and became part of Britain's backbone, the anchor of the Nation's fight to survive on the home front.

It began again in June 1939, and by the time war had been declared three months later, the Land Army had one thousand members. Within two years, that figure had risen to over twenty thousand, peaking to eighty thousand women employed on the land by 1943.

The disruption to trade routes and the attacks on sea convoys had reduced Britain's opportunities to import food from abroad. At home, the bombing of towns and cities affected food production and processing. Many workers had either been called up for the Armed Services or had already left the land for better-paid jobs in factories.

It was clear that a way had to be found to feed the nation if it was to stand any chance of survival. According to an article in 'The Land Girl', the aim was to produce two out of every three meals eaten in Britain, but forty-seven million meals per day would still have to be imported from overseas. This would tie up ships and men who could be otherwise deployed.

As well as producing food, women worked in the forests, felling trees and sawing wood. They tended animals in the fields, cleared and ploughed land for cultivation, cut hedges as an anti-invasion precaution, and cleared ditches.

Over one thousand women were specifically employed to catch rats. In a report in The Times in May 1943, it was noted that over six hundred women were already employed and "their work is stated to be remarkably good."

Later, The Times rather patronisingly admitted that women, after all, were actually quite capable workers who could be trusted.

'With a total strength of sixty thousand, the Women's Land Army is developing fast. No-one now questions the capacity of women to give most valuable help in the food production campaign, which reaches a new peak this year with a further large increase in tillage cropping. Indeed, the demand for the services of women seems likely to continue for some time to outrun the numbers made available by the Ministry of Labour.'

After the war, rationing continued as the country recovered. Many women stayed on and continued their wartime jobs. Others joined up to meet the new challenge of helping Britain back to its feet. The Land Army was finally disbanded in 1950.

To All Land Girls From an admirer of their work

I saw a Land Girl working,
Alone, in an open field.
Her hard, once elegant hands,
A stalwart hoe did wield.
Her back was bent as she slew the weeds
That spoiled the potatoes' growth;
She never wilted, she never paused,
She had taken her silent oath.
At last the day was nearly done,
The sun was sinking low,
She gathered up her jacket,
Then slowly cleaned her hoe.
She passed the chair where I sat,
(I am feeble in body and sight)
She smiled at me as she said:
" Been hot today. Good night."
We hear the valiant deeds of our men
In " furrin parts",
Deeds which bring tears to our eyes,
A glow of pride to our hearts -
But when the war is over and peace at last restored
I shall always remember the Land Girl,
Who made her hoe a sword.

Anon.

CHAPTER FOUR

Daisy Lodge - Timber Corps

Just before war broke out, fourteen year-old Daisy Lodge started work as a messenger girl for a publishing company in London. Born and brought up in Stepney, east London, she had never been on holiday, or to the country - unless you counted Hackney Marshes. World War Two was to change all that and give Daisy the best four years of her life.

In 1941, Daisy decided she wanted to do war work. But there was a problem; she was only sixteen. Undaunted, she added two years to her age and joined a lesser-known part of the Land Army - the Women's Timber Corps.

One very cold Boxing Day, her father took her and a friend to Paddington Station and put them on the train for Hereford and the forestry camp. They were billeted to a village. If the country was a change for Daisy, then Eardisley was even more so.

'I was used to the East End. This was a tiny little place about two to three miles from Hereford. All it had was a pub, a railway station and this big saw mill.'

Daisy was one of five Timber Corps girls there. They all worked in the sawmill with Belgian and Finnish internees. Their job was to measure the cut up timber hewn from trees felled in the nearby forests.

'What we were measuring - we didn't know at the time, was thousands and thousands of coffin boards. We used to measure them and stack them. It's only now that I realise how many people must have been killed during the war. We were only one mill and we made so many - it just makes me think how many other mills must have been doing the same thing.'

After two years, her life changed again. Americans arrived in the next field, distracting Daisy and her friends into fraternising when they should have been sawing. They all got sacked and, as a result, she transferred to a hostel in Hereford, where there were thirty women, two to a room.

Her job also changed. Every morning at 6 o'clock she went into the forest, where timber had already been felled. Then she shackled the trunks to cart-horses and dragged the timber out into the clearing, measured and sawed the logs into smaller lengths with a hand cross cut saw and stacked them to one side for collection. It was hard work.

'There was no electric in those days. We just sawed it by hand, just got on with it. We didn't really think any thing of it.'

Another of Daisy's tasks was cutting hazel branches.

'We had to go into the forest and cut these thin branches and twigs. They were used as mats on landing craft - you know when they have to have something to put over the pebbles so they can get stuff off. Well, we cut all that too.'

Later on in the war, the Timber Corps women were

joined by prisoners of war.

'Italians and Germans started turning up - all prisoners - and they were absolutely flabbergasted that us women were doing this heavy work. They used to help us quite a bit - they'd carry the timber and pile it up for us. They didn't like to see us do that.'

Despite the enjoyment of being outside and in the country, life was very hard for the women. It was physically demanding work and Daisy was poorly fed.

'The landlady at the hostel used to give us breakfast, but we had to find our own dinner. These prisoners used to help us with the food. They'd go and trap rabbits and we used to pick mushrooms and cook them over a fire in the woods. We got a bit of tea back at the hostel but that was it.'

It was also hard financially.

'We only got twenty-five shillings and out of that we had to pay fifteen shillings board and lodging. Luckily, there weren't any shops or anything in them to buy.'

Despite the hardship, Daisy enjoyed her years with the Corps.

'I had the best time. It was my teenage years and we used to go all over the place to dances and the like. There were loads of Americans and they always had food, and a load of British soldiers arrived towards the end. We didn't know who they were at the time, or what they did. They were all really fit. I found out later that they were the first SAS boys.'

Later she became engaged to an American soldier and remembers seeing him leave for the D-Day landings.

'We stayed up all night, waving goodbye to the boys as

they left. And it was goodbye, too, because my American never came back. He was killed.'

After the war, Daisy went back to her old job in publishing.

'I was quite sad in a way that it was all over but it had finished and that part of my life was over. I was still only young. I went back to publishing in Fleet Street and loved every minute of it.'

She also moved back to Stepney.

'My brothers and sisters were all evacuated, but Mother and Dad were there all during the war. They got bombed out and had to move house but it was just a way of life. We'd been bombed and rationed for so long, it was just the way things were.'

Daisy now lives in East Sussex

CHAPTER FIVE

Margaret Bellingham - Land Army

According to the women who served in it, the Land Army offered countless opportunities, not only for new experiences, but also as a means of overcoming shyness and escaping a life that appeared to have been mapped out for them by social expectations.

Margaret Bellingham was not a healthy child. By early adulthood she had already endured several operations. When she decided to join the Land Army, her mother doubted she would pass the medical.

'"Do you good" was the medic's verdict. My grandparents on both sides had had farming connections and the Land Army appealed to me.'

Even the uniform failed to deter her.

'Those awful breeches, pullover and hat! I was sent to Plumpton Agricultural College in Sussex and on my first morning, I was sent off to learn how to milk a cow.'

Despite her optimism, the cow did not turn out to be quite what Margaret had been expecting.

'How naive to imagine we would be let loose on a real cow! It was a trestle with a rubber bag sporting four teats. The bag was filled with water and then 'milked' out.

When it was empty, we filled it up and milked again. By the end of the session we had stiff fingers but we were guaranteed to be able to milk any cow!'

Now fully trained, she was sent to work on a real farm - with real animals.

'Some girls went to farms in gangs, others were sent singly. I was sent off by myself to a farm in Sussex, where the staff consisted of the farmer, his wife and a nephew, plus a lad who was slightly mentally handicapped. There was also a cowman; he lived separately in a house in the village.'

Margaret's hours were long, dictated by the jobs that had to be done. At times, when governed by double summertime, the days seemed endless. The clocks were altered to allow more daylight hours in which to tend the land, but in summer the extra light meant very short nights - and very little sleep.

'It was very light until very late. We worked really long hours especially at harvest time. But regardless of the time we finished, we still had to be up early for milking. But even so, before we could milk, it was my job to get the cows in.'

Breakfast came later and, despite being in the country, Margaret remembers that the food was disappointing.

'The food was awful. Everything seemed to taste of paraffin, no doubt because it was cooked on an ancient paraffin stove.'

The conditions under which the women worked were often determined by the attitude of the farmer towards them. Being on her own, Margaret was perhaps more vulnerable than she would have been had she had a few

Land Army colleagues with her. Now, she questions the motives that drove some farmers.

'The regulations specified we had time off but, despite this, it rarely happened. Looking back, there's no doubt that many Land Army girls were exploited.'

With her health restored, Margaret met the man she was to marry.

'I met him on the farm and I continued to work there until I became pregnant.'

CHAPTER SIX

Barbara Dunlop - Land Army

As one of the most popular occupations for women during the Second World War, the Land Army only received recognition for its wartime contribution much later. As Hitler tried to starve Britain into submission, the Government responded by turning more land over to food production.

Barbara Dunlop from Bognor Regis was nearly eighteen when she joined the Land Army in January 1944. She and her friend Betty were placed in a hostel near Horsham in West Sussex, issued with a bicycle, a black oilskin raincoat, breeches and boots, and sent off to dig for victory.

'We had to get up very early and then we cycled to where the job was. Sometimes it was nearby but other times it was a good hard ride away. Then we worked in the fields all day before cycling back to the hostel.'

The work was physically demanding and very different from what she had been used to.

'I had worked for Boots the chemists behind the cosmetic stand, so all this was new to me. We'd be sent out in the morning with just a few sandwiches to keep us going - they were usually bread and dripping. But one woman we worked for used to take those for her chickens and give us a meal instead, so that was quite nice.'

It was work that both she and Betty loved, even though the conditions were less than luxurious.

'The worst bit was that there were no toilets in the fields. Well, you had to go and so you had to improvise. It was quite a shock at first.'

It could be somewhat awkward on a bicycle, too, even for a proficient rider.

'We used to go around the lanes and quite often you'd meet big Army trucks. They'd just go thundering past and the roads were very narrow, so it was a bit close sometimes.'

The Land Army was also responsible for 'hedging'. With the invasion expected, women were sent out to cut down all the hedges, bushes and trees to shoulder height. Then, if the Germans did invade, they would have little cover. Even when the threat had passed, the hedges were kept at their new level.

These changes to the landscape created another danger to those working in the fields; they could be seen clearly from the sky and were obvious targets for enemy planes. Unlike those in the towns, they had no warning of approaching aircraft.

'Out in the fields there were no sirens and you wouldn't hear them anyway because of the noise of the tractors. We just used to hope that the Germans would ignore us and carry on to where they were going. It wasn't very nice for the people living in the towns but at least they had shelters and a bit of warning.'

Barbara started her Land Army career as an ordinary worker.

'We were W.A, War Agriculture, so we just went where we were sent. That could mean threshing, or digging or anything. After a while, Betty and I decided we wanted to be tractor drivers, so that's what we became.'

She has vivid memories of the first field she ploughed.

'It had just been cleared of trees and was due to be planted with quick-growing food. Well, I'd only get a couple of yards before the tractor would hit a stump, go right up in the air and break the shear on the plough. So I had to keep getting off, fixing it, then setting off again only to have it happen right again.'

Before long the Land Army women were accepted on merit. Barbara and thousands like her toiled day after day, doing men's work in all weathers, in exchange for just two pounds a week.

Despite the harsh conditions, many who worked on the land believed they had a good life and, for Barbara, at least, it gave her confidence. From a painfully shy girl who blushed at the slightest thing, she suddenly became an independent young woman doing important work and coping more than adequately with whatever tasks she was given.

'I was the youngest of seven children, I'd been brought up just to accept what came my way. So I suppose lots of things in the Land Army didn't come as a surprise. I'd had so many hand-me downs in my life that the Land Army clothes were nothing different. But it really helped me out, made me stand up for myself. Mind you, the bikes were pretty ropey.'

With the ever-present fear of being attacked from the

skies, Barbara recalls only one incident where she actually fled in panic. However, it was not fear of the Luftwaffe ,but something far more menacing.

'Betty and I were ploughing away and she was in front. I was aware of where she was but I was also watching what I was doing. Suddenly, I saw her stop, jump off the tractor and run off up the field. It took me a couple of seconds to realise what was going on, then I saw the problem. She'd ploughed straight through a wasps' nest and they were all out to get her. I'd caught up with her tractor by then, so I jumped off too, and ran as fast as I could. I could cope with bullets but not wasps!'

When the war finished, rationing continued. For most Land Army girls de-mobilisation came later. Many wanted to stay on but Barbara was released in March 1946. There was no bitterness.

'There were no perks. We had to give all our clothing back - except the hat and arm band, which was a lot of good! But we had nothing - we'd spent all our time working so we had very little in the way of clothes and shoes. But we didn't get de-mob clothes like the men did. I got twenty and a half extra clothing coupons as a reward for two and a half years working all hours on the land and in all weathers.'

Yet like many of the women of her generation, she had no expectations.

'That was just the way things were then. The men had been fighting and we just picked up their jobs. It was only later when I looked back that I thought: "Oi, what about us girls - we were there too!"'

Only much later did the Land Army receive official

recognition, and were included in the Remembrance Day parades. Until then, thousands of women like Barbara had merely slipped back quietly into civilian life, just as they had slipped into war work during the six long years of fighting.

Barbara now lives in West Sussex.

CHAPTER SEVEN

Barbara Hooper - Land Army

In 1943, Barbara Hooper was eighteen. She was called up for war work and chose to work on the land.

'I didn't fancy munitions at all, so the Land Army was it. When I went along to the office to join up, the woman asked me what I liked doing. So for some odd reason I told her I liked working with horses. I don't know why I said that, as I knew nothing about them at all and as I discovered later, it didn't make any difference anyway!'

Having expressed her interest, Barbara's first job was a related, if unexpected, task; muckspreading.

'I don't know if it was horse muck or cow's muck or anything else muck, but I was given a big fork and told to get on with it. I didn't really know what to do. I mean I'd been working in the Borough Treasurer's office up until then and hadn't a clue. So I just forked the stuff up and threw it around. It wasn't long before I had a lovely line of blisters across my palms!'

Barbara was part of an experimental group of Land Army women. They were known as War Agriculture - War Ag. for short - and its members had specific parameters.

'We had a seven mile limit. We were given these War

Ag. bikes and got sent off on jobs, but only up to a maximum of seven miles away. It was all contract work and we were billeted in cottages.'

The gang was involved with hedging when the invasion was expected. It was a very unpopular job with the women.

'It was so terribly itchy. Everything had to be cut off at eye level so that we could see the Germans coming, which they never did of course, but everything had to be cut down in case they did.'

It was during this time she discovered she was something of a pyromaniac.

'We had to burn all the rubbish and I turned out to be very good at starting fires. So I'd get sent off and I'd walk to a farm, get a bale of straw and some paraffin and walk back and light it. I was good at that - and it meant time away from that awful hedging!'

The fires also came in handy for cooking their meals, especially during the winter months. With all day spent in the fields, the cold was almost crippling.

'We'd be out lifting sugar beet when the sugar was on the leaf - that meant with snow and frost on them and we'd put sacks over our heads and shoulders for warmth. The landlady would give us raw potatoes and we'd take them with us and cook them in the embers of the fires that we lit. At least it gave us a hot meal - even if there wasn't very much of it!'

The experimental group was disbanded in the spring of 1944 and Barbara was reassigned to an arable farm.

'My friend and I decided we wanted to run a chicken farm after the war so he said I should go to a real farm. I ended up on one that had chickens and crops - and a very odd family who owned it'.

The farmer was a committed Baptist. His daughter, however, resented his strictures. Whilst the farmer seemed mostly unaware of her behaviour, Barbara was frequently confronted with evidence of her rebellion.

'The daughter was having it off with the sheep man and I kept stumbling across their clinches - which usually took place in the incubation shed for some odd reason. Then she liked Black Cat cigarettes and I had to pretend that I knew nothing about that either!'

Her ability to keep her opinions to herself meant she was left alone to get on with her work, and make use of whatever opportunities came her way.

'I used to go in on a Sunday to feed the hens and there would be eggs stacked up and ready to go off to be rationed. Quite often there'd be double-yoked eggs there which I got very good at spotting. So I used to pinch them and take them home to my mother.'

Life on the land was hard but, apart from getting shot at, it was a relatively steady existence. Yet every so often Barbara came come across things that betrayed an almost quaint simplification of the effect of a world at war.

'Where I was billeted at this cottage, the landlady was a sweet little old lady. Her nephew had come home from Burma and he had had a bad time there. He was billeted somewhere nearby and one night she called me and asked me to walk him up the lane. She explained that she needed me to do that because, "He isn't used to the blackout dear." I mean, he'd survived all that time in Burma in terrible conditions and there she was worried about him getting lost in the blackout!'

CHAPTER EIGHT

Cecilia Rockliffe

Whilst the overall effect of the Second World War was devastating nationally, it set many people on a path which they maintained for the rest of their lives.

Cecilia Rockliffe was one of six children from Shirley, near Croydon. When war was declared, she was evacuated to Hove, near Brighton, on the south coast. She remembers being billeted there with her younger sister, Jean, who was then six. Cecilia was fourteen.

'My mother came to see us but we were quite happy. It was just like an extended holiday in many ways. And I was with my sister. But then they started talking about the invasion, and things changed a bit.'

No-one could have foreseen that, with the fall of France, the German front line would be just twenty miles away across the English Channel.

'Looking back now, it seems ridiculous to send people nearer to the Germans but that was what happened. I suppose it was a question of just getting us out of the city where we would definitely be in danger, or getting us away and hoping for the best.'

The South East was a prime target for enemy aircraft.

'We lived very near to Croydon and so we were right on

top of some places that the Germans wanted to attack - there was Croydon Airport as well as RAF Kenley, and Redhill airfield. So my mother wanted us somewhere safe.'

With an invasion believed imminent, the evacuation process began again. This time it was inland but still away from the big cities.

'My sister and I were sent from Hove to Virginia Water in Surrey, and then for a while to Guildford. After that we came out to the country.'

The chore of finding somewhere to stay was difficult, especially where siblings had to be accommodated.

'I can remember walking around the streets with a teacher and I had my sister Jean with me. We wanted to stay together and I remember thinking, "Will nobody take us?" It was horrible. We kept going from house to house and got nearer and nearer to the end of the road, but then we eventually got a place to stay.'

As the war continued, Cecilia moved again.

'I went to the farm - right out in the country and I learned to milk a goat. That was it really, I loved it. It was a wonderful opportunity, and I still often think how lucky I was.'

In fact, it made such a big impression on her that as soon as she was old enough, she joined the Land Army.

'It was the start of my life really, when I came to Surrey. I looked out of the window onto all this beautiful countryside and was thankful for it. It was as if I had always been here - and I never went back to Shirley.'

Although Cecilia recalls her days on the land with affection, she also remembers some of the drawbacks, particularly the primitive conditions.

'I lived and worked on a farm and I had come from a home in Shirley where we were all very well looked after, so some of it was a bit of a shock. The loo was in the corner of the woodshed - and there was no loo paper of course. It was squares of newspaper hanging from a nail on the side. And there was no heating in the bedrooms. We had to break the ice on the water in the winter so that we could wash. But I loved it. I really did.'

The benefits of her new life far outweighed the discomforts.

'I used to love milking. We had to get up very early of course and it was always freezing, but I loved the cosiness of the stall. Cows are very warm animals and they are gentle. We milked by hand - no electric in those days.'

In fact, the cow stall was so cosy that it was not unknown for people to be affected by the rhythmic sounds of the milking process.

'The cowman was called Vic and he had always worked on the farm. When we used to do the milking, we each sat next to a cow on one of those little stools and we'd milk away. We'd chat of course, and quite often I'd say something and get no reply, and realise that a there was no squirting noise because Vic had dropped off and was leaning against the cow. So I'd call out to him, "Vic, have you gone to sleep?" and then the squirt, squirt would start again.'

And Cecilia was well-nourished.

'We had proper food in those days - no snacks or sweets - and we worked very hard, so we were fit and well-fed. But we also had our fun, too. It was during this time that I paid my first visit to a pub, although I never told my mother as I don't think that she would have been too pleased. And that was how I met my husband - in a pub!'

During the war years, communities changed week by week. Very few of the towns and villages retained their pre-war make up. The constant change meant that newcomers did not remain outsiders for long and soon put down roots. Cecilia, who had already adapted, could appreciate change from both sides.

'I'd been an evacuee and had left my home. Now I had begun again and so I knew what it felt like to be the new person in the village. But I think that we were all very friendly and welcoming. And I remained friends with many people after the war had finished.'

Cecilia stayed in her new home on the Surrey/Sussex border. She still lives there today.

CHAPTER NINE

Kay O'Neill - Land Army

Kay O'Neill was one of three children. Her brother had a farm near Newbury, and she was with him when war was declared.

'I was twenty-one and I missed my party because of it. I made a decision not to join the Land Army as we thought the war would be over in six months.'

A few months later, when her brother joined the RAF, a neighbouring farmer offered her work. With three farms ranging over thirteen hundred acres, he needed someone who could not only use the farm machinery but was experienced with animals. With petrol on short supply, Kay would be able to use her own horse as transport to check cattle on the outlying farms. As the war began in earnest, she accepted his offer, not least because some of her own resources had begun to dwindle.

'I gradually wore out my own clothes and for the sake of becoming uniformed, I had to join the Land Army to get something to wear. It seemed a practical decision. I had no coupons to replace them and the Land Army provided us with very hard-wearing work gear. We all thought the war would be of very short duration, and I went into it as a temporary measure.'

Unlike many Land Army women, she remained close to home.

'I was based at Yattendon, six miles from my brother's farm. I didn't have to lose my neighbours and friends. It all seemed rather convenient.'

She had previously worked with horses and dogs and knew the routines of farm life well.

'I was experienced with modern milking machines and so when our herdsman went to join the Army, I was useful for the milking in the morning.

The work was hard and the days long, but Kay enjoyed it.

'I felt physically very well. It didn't come as a tremendous hardship to me, like other girls who'd perhaps worked in London. On the whole, I found it was what I wanted to do. And it was a pleasant way of working during the war.'

Gradually, other women arrived. As the senior land girl, Kay had to show them what to do and how to do it.

'To start with there was just me and one other girl, Doris Jeffries. She had been a hairdresser in London and found it very hard going. By the end of the war, there were four of us. They had lots of guts. The worse thing we had to contend with, though, was the men being rather unpleasant to us. They always resented us women.'

Unpleasant or not, the women worked alongside the men, harvesting, haymaking, milking and riding out to check on the herds. They were not well-paid.

'I was paid something like eighteen shillings a week at the beginning of the war but towards the end it was forty-five shillings, normally without overtime. I paid my landlady twenty-five shillings a week of that and, of course, pay-as-you-earn. But we didn't think about the money, we just knew we had to stick to the job and just do it, not grumble.'

Although Kay preferred her life on the land to a job in a factory, but there were occasions when the open air proved more of a risk than an idyll. The threat from the air was ever present.

'During harvest one year I was building the load on top of a cart with a man leading the horse. All of a sudden, the sky became dark with aircraft. The men all took cover under the hedges, leaving me on top of the load. However, I managed to slip down and calm the horse as the aircraft went over. The animals were just as scared as we were when the bombs fell. The bombs looked just like strings of sausages.'

Then there were the hazards more usually associated with life on a farm. Early one morning, as she rounded up the cows for milking, Kay almost died.

'I fell into a liquid cesspit. There was no guard rail and I fell in. My wellington boots dragged me down and I would have drowned had it not been for a clump of very woody stinging nettles that I managed to hang onto until the cowman rescued me. It was a very frightening moment.'

The farmer had removed the barbed wire from around the pit after one of the young cows had torn its udder on it. Nobody thought to tell the Land Girls, but despite her ordeal, Kay met with very little sympathy.

'I stripped down in the outside shed, washed myself with freezing cold water and then went straight back to work. All the farmer could say was, "Look at that filth on my new car seat!" I thought it was a bit much really!'

On another morning, despite a septic big toe, with her foot heavily swathed in bandages, she was on her way to cut some hay when she heard a noise behind her.

'The bull had been in all winter and had just been released. It was rushing down the field, straight towards me, kicking its hind legs in the air as it went. My word, I forgot about septic feet as I tore round the other side of the haystack, just in time for the bull's horns to get stuck in it. I escaped into a nearby wood but, my God, my foot was agony afterwards!'

Like many of her contemporaries, Kay remembers the war years as exceptional times. Times of sharing, hardship and shortages.

'I liked the feeling of togetherness. We borrowed, swapped and lent clothes. I can remember lending my pretty nightdress that my brother had sent me from America. It went on honeymoon with at least half a dozen of my friends.'

That sense of camaraderie continued after the war. When she was invited to a special reception, friends rallied round.

'It was a garden party at Buckingham Palace and I was invited because I had the record as the longest serving landgirl in Berkshire. I was about five years working on the farm, and off I went in all my friends' clothes, to eat thin cucumber sandwiches with the King and Queen. Of course, it wasn't quite like that. I was a bit disappointed that I only saw them from a distance.'

Then there were the airmen.

'I was very fortunate to be in Yattendon because there were dances there. And at Hampstead Norreys we had the American Air Force who were always good for a Saturday night hop. We had hops in the village hall and hops in neighbouring Chieveley. We used to cycle as much as six or seven miles each way to get to a dance, as that was our main source of entertainment.

Despite her mostly happy memories of the war years, Kay was touched by tragedy when her fiancé was killed in North Africa. But the world had become used to death and her request for a day off did not find favour.

'I wanted to go and see his parents when I got the news. Their other son had already been killed, but when I asked my boss, he said, "No." We were short of staff and I was told that if I went, I need not come back. So, of course, I remained at my post in the milking parlour. I felt very sad that day.'

Kay married after the war, ran a riding school in Malaya and raised two children. She now lives in East Sussex.

CHILDREN

Very few people remained unaffected by the Second World War. Even the children lived their lives around it, often playing a greater part than would normally be expected.

With their schooling disrupted, their families fragmented and their world in turmoil, they simply followed the adults - and did war work.

CHAPTER TEN

Betty Waters - Child

'We spent the school holidays on the farm. My mother always worked on the land, even before the war, so it was just what we did - me and Betty Jackson. They lived a couple of doors down and Mrs Jackson worked with my mum. She was the overseer, but the Jackson's were quite well-off by our standards. They had a piano and Betty had a bicycle.'

Betty Waters had just received a scholarship to Maidstone Girls Grammar School when the declaration of war was made. From a poor, working-class family, her scholarship was a cause for concern to her mother.

'Dad was out of work and Mum earned what she could along the farm. All three of my brothers were off fighting and the oldest one was a POW. Poor old Mum had to work herself silly to earn money to send him food and then I got this place at the Grammar and needed a uniform. Well, we had to pay for it somehow. We didn't even have anything we could flog to get money, so I had to work with her - it was piece work and that's how I got my uniform. I was ten.'

Both Betty and her friend were used to farm life. Living

so close to each other, they had grown up doing jobs with their mothers.

'The farm was just along the road and at the start of the war we did get let off the hard jobs, so we used to ride Betty's bike round the yard. It was summer 1941, and I think that's what we were doing when this plane came over.'

Edmunds' Farm in Barming slopes down to the River Medway. Much of the land is still the same - orchards full of the apple trees and pears that epitomise Kent. But during the war, the orchards were also planted with other food crops - potatoes, cabbages, peas, beans, swedes and turnips. There was one tractor, but no petrol, so it was only utilised for special jobs. Generally, they used horses.

As the overseer, Betty's mother, Flo' looked after the animals and acted as chief cart driver. She had just taken one of the big horses into the shed, when Betty recalls hearing shouts from the field.

'The yard was on the top bit of the farm, not far from the road. Mum was in the shed and me and Betty were sitting on a couple of old boxes. I can remember it so clearly; we were sitting in the sun. Some of the women were in the first field and they started shouting. We didn't notice at first, but we did when Mum came running out of the shed.'

'She ran to the edge of the field and looked up. So we went to see what was going on. There was this plane, on its own, and it was really low. We saw planes every day - they were usually Germans and they often shot us, but this one wasn't the same. And he wasn't shooting. He was going slow and he was going towards the river but he couldn't seem to turn.'

The plane was an Italian fighter and it had been hit in the rudder. Unable to steer, the pilot was looking for a place to crash land.

'Mum was shouting. She had a voice like a foghorn. And she was waving her arms about. One of the women ran off to the house while the others started to run after the plane - it was very low by this time and looked like it would crash before it got to the river - and that was only two fields away. Meanwhile, Mum got on this horse. She must've unhitched it, and the next thing, her and this woman called Ida were on it, and after the plane. Well, this horse didn't want to know. Mum was yelling at it and poking it and they got past the others, but next thing they jumped off and ran towards the water.'

The River Medway is only about ten yards wide at this point and the opposite bank was lined with a shallow wood of alder and willow trees, at most fifteen feet tall.

'Mum and Ida had sticks, rakes probably, and the plane was only just above the trees. Me and Betty started to run as well but the farmer appeared and told us to go back to the yard. He ran after them, so we got on Betty's bike and rode round the track to the river. That's how we saw where the plane landed. It got across the water OK and scraped the trees the other side. He landed just past them, only about thirty yards from the water.'

The woman who had run to the house when the plane first appeared had raised the alarm. As soon as the pilot landed his crippled plane, a policeman and a Home Guard appeared beside it. Some of the women jumped in the river and splashed across. Flo' Waters was one of them.

'I remember them all running up to the water's edge and Mum kept going, she just sort of ran across the water. And so did Ida. It was amazing. Just as well it was summer - they only had breeches and tops on, but they scrambled up the bank the other side and ran through the trees. Neither of them could swim.'

The Italian pilot was unhurt and was taken away. The women stayed by the plane until help arrived. According to Betty, the pilot had a lucky escape.

'I wouldn't have fancied his chances if Mum had got there first. All of these women had somebody who was fighting, so who knows what would have happened? But I do remember she used to say, "They're all someone's son."

It was that reality that stayed with Betty, although she had her own reasons for feeling cheered by the spectacle. Whilst enemy airmen may well have been someone's son, the captured ones could not hurt her brothers.

'I remember gangs of prisoners working on the land or on the streets during the war. They were young and I remember some embarrassed me once by talking to me as I walked home from school. I was about fifteen and I decided that, as I could speak a bit of German, I'd tell them off. I said something like, "Don't speak to me, I'm English and you're our prisoners." One of them said, "Not for long. We're Germans and one day you'll be ours." I remember being quite shocked. I don't know if it was because he'd understood my German, or because he spoke to me in English, but it taught me to keep my opinions to myself.'

While Betty may have guarded her opinions, she still looked on the prisoners with a mixture of curiosity and pity. One winter, she watched from her home as a group of them cleared the snow.

'They were just outside our house. It was really cold. I felt sorry for them, they weren't much older than me. Mum was out working, so I pinched a currant loaf from the kitchen and gave it to one of them. I remember him looking at me, then smiling as he took it. Maybe he thought I'd poisoned it, or something.'

It was sobering coming face-to-face with those responsible for disrupting daily life. Whilst they became accustomed to the planes high above dropping their bombs and strafing civilians, it was still disturbing to see captured airmen up close. For Betty Waters, who spent most of her schooldays in air-raid shelters, it is something she remembers vividly.

'I used to walk to school through the raids. We just did. In the summer, I remember looking up at the sky and seeing the dog-fight trails. I used to wonder what the pilots looked like. Mum used to say they looked the same as us but it was only when prisoners started showing up, I realised she was right.'

Even school children became used to the sounds of war.

'We got so used to it that we never really took much notice. At first, we were in the classrooms but then they put sandbags right up the windows, so there was only a gap at the top. It only let in a bit of light so it was always dim inside. When the siren went off, we just lined up and filed out quickly, never running, and went down the shelter. It was damp and smelly down there but at least we had electric light.'

They became so accustomed to this routine that even

when their exams were interrupted, the girls knew what to do.

'The siren would go off, we put our pencils down, lined up quickly, definitely no talking, straight down to the shelters to our places. Then the teacher would appear. She'd picked up our papers and pencils and she'd give them out and we'd carry on as if nothing had happened. Each class had its own place and we knew where to go. Ours was round a couple of zig-zags - they were to stop the blast. I don't how we'd have got out if we'd been hit. There was only one entrance as I remember.'

Another vivid memory is of seeing a bomber over the town. It flew over her house before unleashing its deadly cargo.

'It dropped a string, just like you see in the films. I was playing with Betty Jackson up her alley when I saw my mother go running past, looking for me. I called out to her and she was so relieved to see me that she shouted at me. Then she made me go back to the farm with her.'

Others had not been so lucky. Detling Airfield was a fighter station just to the south of Maidstone. There had been a raid on it earlier and the lone bomber had probably got separated from its squadron. The damage was massive and was graphically reported in 'The Kent Messenger.'

'A lot of WAAF's got killed. They'd hit the shelters and I remember seeing pictures of loads and loads of legs sticking out of the ground. It was all the dead WAAF's.'

Betty Waters still lives near Maidstone.

CHAPTER ELEVEN

Marion Wormull - Child

September 1939 was a turning point for five year-old Marion Wormull from West Malling in Kent. Not only was she poised to start school that month and begin the transition from infant to child, but her rural home was about to become a battle ground.

'We lived in cottages that belonged to Colonel Luck but the orchards and meadow belonged to Eden Farm.'

On the other side of the farm was West Malling Aerodrome - and the Royal Air Force. Only a mile from Marion's home, West Malling Aerodrome was to become one of the most prominent RAF fighter stations of the Second World War. The Spitfire and Hurricane squadrons based on the other side of the fruit trees were the outer ring of defence for London.

'I remember nothing of World War Two actually starting. I do know that for a long time we would have our wireless on for all the news broadcasts. People would talk about what was happening in Poland, but it all seemed so far away.'

That remote feeling soon faded as the war became part of Marion's life. Brick air-raid shelters were built in the schoolyard and in the town square. Sandbags surrounded doorways, and railings were cut down and taken away for smelting into guns and aircraft. The windows of her cottage were criss-crossed with white tape and draped with black curtains.

'I remember learning about gas at school and being cautioned about light. That's why we had to draw the curtains before any lamp could be lit indoors - even the light of a cigarette could be seen from the air.'

Gas masks became a necessary yet cumbersome accessory.

'We carried them over our shoulders at all times, in a brown canvas type box with a strap. Men had much larger ones, which looked scary and some of the really young children had colourful ones that looked like Mickey Mouse. We were taught in school how to use our gas masks and they would bring mobile gas units around for us to check if they were airtight.'

Apart from gas, there was the ever-present danger of explosions.

'We were warned not to pick up anything off the street even if it looked pretty, because it could be a bomb and might blow us up.'

Being in the midst of the Kent countryside, Marion soon noticed an influx of people from outside the area. There were soldiers billeted in nearby Manor Park, now an Army camp.

'I remember the Nissan huts all over the park, with their arching corrugated tin roofs. The grass was churned up by large Army vehicles that also turned the peaceful country lanes into noisy, muddy thoroughfares. The serenity was all gone in an instant it seemed. The large manor house was used as a convalescent home for wounded soldiers, sailors and airmen.'

Then there was the Land Army.

'I remember them clearly because they all wore dark green boots.'

Her own family did their bit.

'Dad worked on the railway and he was too old to join up, so he joined the Home Guard. Mum and Aunt Diddy worked in a factory making metal bits and pieces and they both hated it.'

However, some of her neighbours intrigued the young Marion.

'The two ladies next door received disability pay but they would dig in their garden for hours and do really heavy work. If somebody came by they would race into the house so as not to be seen working and lose their allowance. They kept this up until they were old but they were very strong and did work that other people would need a man to do.'

There were also the two girls who had been billeted on their family. Sisters who had been evacuated from Woolwich, in south east London.

'They were both nice girls. One was younger than me and had bright red hair. Dad called her carrots but her real name was Lily Semple. Her sister was called Marjorie. I don't remember too much about them as they didn't stay with us long, but I do remember that they were poor - even poorer than us. They didn't have many clothes, so Mum gave them some of ours.'

After about a year of war, things changed once again for Marion.

'At first, there was nothing much happening in the country. But after our evacuees left, the bombing became worse. To start with it was just at night and when the sirens went off, we'd scramble out of bed and go into a cupboard or closet until the all clear went. Sometimes if it wasn't too bad, we'd stay in bed.'

This was the Blitz and Marion was living next to a major airfield.

'Often the planes would drone over our house on their way to London and leave us pretty much alone. But other times they would try to hit the fighter and bombers up at the airfield. We would hear the planes revving-up and watch the dog-fights overhead.'

She was soon able to distinguish one aircraft from another.

'The German planes sounded very different from ours. We had mainly Spitfires, Hurricanes and Mosquitoes and some bombers near us. The German planes, mainly Messerschmidts, Dorniers and Heinkels had an undulating drone. We had a cat once called Messerschmidt - it was because he purred so loudly and sounded just like a plane.'

Aircraft recognition was considered essential learning for children. They had to know what was friendly and what was not. They could also provide valuable information for the authorities.

'We once had a plane identification competition at school. There were several pages of pictures and some pictures of parts like wings and things. We had to identify them. I won a new identity bracelet with my name and address engraved on it and a nice leather strap. They were so the ARP could identify us.'

Before long, the raids came both day and night.

'We spent hours in the shelters listening to the bombs whistling down and the gunfire noise. We used to sing to drown out the noise and stop us from getting too scared. Sometimes it was deafening with the bombs dropping and planes fighting overhead and the anti-aircraft guns booming away.'

Even after it was over, the uncertainty remained. It affected everybody, and for those parents who had to entrust their children into the care of teachers, it was particularly worrying.

'We never knew when we came out of school if we had a home or even parents to go back to. And our poor parents never knew if the school had been hit and the children blown to pieces or buried under rubble. One morning a boy called Teddy - he was my age - didn't come to school. His house had suffered a direct hit the evening before and his mother had thrown herself over him. She was killed instantly and he got head injuries that required him to wear a patch on his head well into adult life.'

Even in quiet periods, the war still intruded.

'The Army installed an anti-aircraft gun in the meadow in front of our house and we had another in the lane leading to the school. One soldier, who was manning the gun in the meadow, drew a picture of our house and gave it to Mum and Dad. But life carried on as normally as possible as the war progressed.'

Soon, it became obvious that their location had become too dangerous and, even if they did live in the middle of the country, Marion and her sister, Thelma, would have to follow in the footsteps of the Semple girls and be evacuated. And if they needed persuasion, there came the moment that brought the whole war home to her.

'One cold Spring night, the siren wailed but there were no bombs dropping. That was unusual. Planes from the airfield had taken off but the droning seemed to go on forever. Dad called us and said, "London is in for it tonight." As we stood by the back door, it was just a black mass of planes droning over our house the sky was full and they looked just like a swarm of locusts blocking out the moonlight. As we watched, over the horizon towards London, we could see it light up and hear the faint sound of bombs dropping as London went up in flames. Wave after wave came over to pound London into the ground.'

To Marion and Thelma the war seemed to go on forever. Days and weeks blurred into one as the fighting carried on.

'We used to lie in bed and wonder if we would still be alive tomorrow. And just when we'd begun to wonder if it would ever end, the doodlebugs started. They were really scary. I used to hate to go to the bathroom when there was an air-raid on. I had visions of sitting on the throne while the side of the house was blasted away, leaving me exposed, or being found dead with my pants down, or perhaps naked in the bath tub. We never did receive a direct hit but the ceiling came down once when a bomb dropped in the orchard nearby. We used to doubt if there was a God but used to say our prayers anyway, just in case there was and he was listening.'

Evacuation came late for the sisters. It was 1944 and Marion remembers being excited by the prospect.

'I remember jumping up and down and telling my mother

we were going to the seaside. It must have been so difficult for her, knowing that we were going somewhere to live with somebody else who none of us knew.'

They were sent off on the train with gas masks, nametags and some sandwiches for the journey.

'It was all secret for security reasons, not even the teachers who were with us knew where we were going. Our parents didn't know our destination either. They just had to trust the authorities to do what was right for their little ones.'

Their destination was a school in Aberystwyth. They they spent the first night on the gym floor before being taken from door-to-door to find a billet.

'The teacher knocked on a door and the house looked good. But when the lady looked us up and down and said she'd take the big one (Thelma) but not the small one (me) she crossed her off the list. The woman only wanted help around the house.'

Whilst efforts were made to keep siblings together, it often proved difficult. Families had their own children to look after and were trying to survive the war just like the evacuees. Marion and Thelma were eventually found lodgings next door to each other.

'My lady had never had children and didn't really have a clue. I got on very well with the man but I was far from happy there. I wasn't keen on the lady - she was nothing like my mother and I believe she felt a little awkward. My sister told me that my lady would complain to her lady about me crying and that she didn't know what to do with me.'

Eventually, Marion and Thelma adapted to their new life

and actually began to discover some benefits.

'We went to school in the chapel and during morning break we would sneak across the road to a bakery and get day-old rolls. We'd tuck them up our knicker leg so the teacher wouldn't find out and then eat them in the toilet. It was the best bread we'd ever tasted. Looking back, we must have been really hungry. Some had wonderful people, others didn't.'

Then there was the freedom. With no parents or relatives around to report on the young evacuees, Marion discovered that being away from home could be good fun.

'We never went out with our ladies, but we'd play with other kids. We'd play in the old castle ruins - even though it was out of bounds - or along the promenade, dodging waves as they came towering over it. One day my lady got very angry with me. She said: "What on earth have you got in your hair, you dirty thing?" It turned out to be seagull droppings. She never did wash my hair while I was there as I remember.'

Ironically, the unpleasant additions to Marion's hair were to be her salvation.

'The nit lady came once and found I had a head full of lice. After that, my lady wanted nothing more to do with me, so she sent me away. I was found another billet - the other side of the town from my sister, with a young policeman and his wife. They had a baby called Geraint; I'd always wanted a brother. I enjoyed my short time with them.'

Unbeknown to Marion, her sister Thelma had written home and informed their parents that as Marion had nits, they should come quickly.

'One day there was a knock at the door and it was Dad. I was pleased to see him, but I was having a good time with my new family and friends and it meant I had to leave them. He must have been disappointed at the reception he got from me but I really wasn't ready to go home. But it was great to see my mother again - but she cried when she saw what they'd done to my hair - they'd chopped it all off really short and uneven because of the nits. It never did grow back nice and wavy again.'

By now, the war had turned and the Allies had control. The Army post in Manor Park was turned into a POW camp, firstly for Italians and then for Germans. This proved a source of intrigue for Marion who was struck by how normal the prisoners appeared.

'Some prisoners worked with Dad on the farms and they used to chat to us and show us pictures of their own children and their wives. They missed them, too. I remembered how, when the bombing was on, I used to think about what they looked like up there and wonder if they were tired or scared. Now I knew they had been - they were just like us.'

Far from being locked away, the prisoners not only worked alongside their captors but also became part of the local community.

'I remember one Sunday at Christmas some Germans came to our church and sat in the middle, in a group. One of the church officials asked them to move to the side, which they did, but they stayed and us children moved to the side with them.'

Many Germans remained in the camp after the war ended, waiting to be repatriated. Some stayed and made a new life in England. Some had no homes or family to go back to.

'Nobody ever wins a war - everyone loses. Don't let anyone tell you otherwise. There's no glory in it.'

Marion now lives in the United States.

CHAPTER TWELVE

Pamela Briant - Evacuee

'I remember my mother arguing with my father about whether I should be sent away or stay with them in London. The war had just started and I was eleven but I can remember it so clearly. Dad said I should go. She said I should stay. I thought it would be an adventure but then I didn't want to miss out on anything either.'

The plan to evacuate children from the big cities had been drawn up months before the war started. It also included mothers with babies, pregnant women and a number of people with disabilities. It turned into a logistical nightmare that left many people deeply unhappy.

Although the motives behind the plan were both good and sensible, it made no allowance for the pain of separation. Nor did it foresee the subsequent problems with host families.

For many parents, the idea of sending their offspring to an unknown place, into the care of strangers, was unthinkable and they refused to let them go.

Pamela Briant has vivid memories of her mother during that time. With her father working away from home, the decision must have caused her great anxiety.

'I was an only child and I went everywhere with Mum

before the war. Dad worked on the railways and he never seemed to be there. I remember that Mum used to creep into my room when she thought I was asleep and sit and look at me. She never said anything and if I woke up, she'd fluff my pillow up and tell me to go back to sleep. I think she was trying to work out what to do with me.'

Parents were well aware that they and their children were living in danger, but did it justify sending them away from all that was familiar?

In the first months of the war, the need for decisive action receded as the Germans failed to materialise. Despite the threat just across the Channel, for many life carried on pretty much as normal.

'Lots of my friends had been evacuated at the start but some had come back, so that was nice. We did have air-raids and that but it wasn't too bad. Mum seemed to be a bit happier, too, and she'd gone back to being herself. Dad was still on the trains then.'

When the Battle of Britain started, things changed once again. With schooling already disrupted, lessons stopped altogether. Finally, Pamela only went to school to borrow books.

Meanwhile, her mother was doing voluntary work at Whipp's Cross Hospital, not far from the family home in Walthamstow.

'I thought that no school would mean more time with friends, but I was so wrong. Mum used to take me with her to the hospital and make me read to the patients. It was her way of making sure I learned - and of keeping an eye on me.'

Before long, Pamela realised that what had started as a

chore was actually a great way to get noticed - and earn some pocket money.

'At first, I hated it until I realised that I could impress people with how much I knew - well, thought I knew. So I'd read to them from my school books but also from the papers and Picture Post. Then somebody asked me to write a letter for him and he gave me tuppence. So after that I was onto a good thing and I charged for a letter writing service!'

The arrangement solved two problems at once. Pamela's mother could now not only keep an eye on her daughter and know she was safe, but she didn't have to pay for childcare, either. And nobody at the hospital seemed to mind.

'I don't suppose I was really supposed to be there, but as I was helping the patients, I think they turned a blind eye. Mum always made sure that the doctors didn't find out though, just in case.'

By the time the Blitz was underway, Pamela's mother decided they should leave London.

'We went up to Cambridgeshire and stayed there for the rest of the war. I think Mum had been up that way before and that's why we went there. She joined the Land Army and we had a room in a big house. I think it must have been a vicarage or something like that. It was in the country so, again, it was quite easy for her to keep me nearby.'

During the working day, while her mother was busy with the farm, Pamela was left to amuse herself.

'I'd made friends and we used to spend our time around the farms, collecting swill and eggs and doing little jobs like that. I think everybody had more or less given up on the idea of school by then, so we just did bits and pieces to help out. It was hard work but I enjoyed it and, although we were still young, we felt we were doing our bit.'

If the days were fun for Pamela, the evenings were even better. Their integration into life in rural Cambridgeshire had been easy and they had found their place in the fledgling community of landgirls and farm workers.

'We used to have get togethers and quite often we'd all eat round one table. We used to make right old feasts although it was nothing special. It was just plain food but everybody put something in. And we'd sing and talk. It was great. Mum was so much happier up there than in London.'

Their removal from the danger of the Capital to the comparative safety of the countryside also conferred a sense of perspective. Their safety was paramount; nothing else mattered.

'She used to say to me that the stuff in the flat where we lived in London was only stuff and not worth worrying about. When we left, we'd taken what we could carry but, like she said, that was all we needed.'

That attitude made the discomforts of their new home more bearable.

'It was very cold up there in the winter, but at least it was safer than London was. Later on, when I'd had my own children, I understood why Mum had been so keen to keep me with her.

Pamela Briant now lives in Northampton.

CHAPTER THIRTEEN

Doris Russell - Child

Coastal England was the destination of many children evacuated from the big inland towns and cities at the beginning of the war. For many children from London, Birmingham and Manchester, this was their first glimpse of the sea.

'We had lots of children from London come to Worthing. We shared our schools with them and they brought their teachers. I remember that boys from the Battersea Grammar School came down.'

Doris Russell from Worthing, West Sussex, was twelve when war broke out. She remembered returning home from Sunday school and hearing the announcement.

'My mother and father were listening to the wireless and I can still remember how I felt when I heard that news, when I heard the words, "This country is at war with Germany." I felt excitement; I didn't really understand what was happening, but the announcement is as clear today as it was then.'

However, her initial excitement was tempered when she learned the truth about rationing.

'I had thought I would get my own little tuck box, with

one egg, a rasher of bacon, a piece of cheese in it and that I would be able to eat it when I wanted. I was looking forward to that until my mother said that all the rations would have to go in together. So that was that!'

Life changed quite dramatically for Doris in those early years. Apart from spending many hours in the air-raid shelters, where they sang songs and danced to pass the time, her house was filled with strangers.

'We had a big five-bedroomed house in Worthing and Mother decided that we could take in some of the London children. So we took in ten or twelve at a time.'

Some evacuees had a very difficult time. They were frequently seen as home help or free labour by some hosts. In some cases, the accommodation provided was inadequate and very basic. However, for the evacuees with Mrs Russell, life was comfortable.

'She was used to keeping a guest house and so was able to manage the rations and make the food go round so that everybody had enough. She did that well. And I would help her with the jobs and things.'

The evacuees were accommodated three to a bedroom, but they lived separately from the host family. It meant that part of her home was no longer open to Doris or her younger brother.

'They shared our schools with us and when they weren't at school, the dining room was their room where they sat and did their homework. But I was never allowed in there except in the evening when I had to help my mother take in a tray of bedtime drinks for them. They had either cocoa or Bovril and I got to help her give them out. I wasn't allowed to speak to them. I could feel myself going red every time but I still thought it was great. I mean, I was twelve and they were boys! But that was the only contact I had with them.'

Things changed on the South Coast when the threat of invasion gained momentum.

'The evacuees gradually started to go; the bombing in London had eased up a bit by then. I don't know if ours went back to London or if they went elsewhere but they went.'

Doris' father and elder brother had both been called up by then, leaving Doris, her mother and her younger brother alone in the house.

'My mother didn't want us to go away, my brother and I. She wanted us to stick together but I do know that she was absolutely dreading an invasion and she used to talk to us about it. I don't know what she was planning but I can remember being frightened at the thought that they would come. We thought we'd rather die than live with it.'

In the meantime, Doris was still attending dancing school. With the threat of invasion came an influx of troops, ready to deal with any Germans who did attempt to set foot in England. Their presence gave Doris and her friend a ready-made audience and an opportunity to contribute to the war effort.

'There were a lot of French Canadians in Worthing and we used to go and entertain them. They were all along the front with their tanks. We did a show and danced on the pier in Worthing I remember. We also danced for the American soldiers who were based over at West Chiltington. They were always very appreciative and we loved doing it. It was great fun.'

By now, Doris was nearly fourteen and about to leave school. Whilst the bombing continued, along the South Coast in particular, hit and run raids by lone German planes were common.

'I was very frightened the whole time. We had a Morrison shelter in the front room and there was just room for my brother and I. We slept in it and Mother slept nearby. When the planes came at night we'd hear them on their way to London and my heart would really beat. I felt so nervous, wondering if they would be intercepted and let go of their bombs.'

On one particular occasion, she had a narrow escape.

'I was still only thirteen and my friend and I were walking to Sunday school when a plane appeared overhead from very low cloud. We stopped and watched it even though we could see the big black crosses and knew it was a German. A milkman shouted, "Get down, flat on the pavement!" and we did. We then heard bombs and they hit a house in Falcombe Street only about fifty yards away. The whole ground shook but we still went to church.'

With her school life disrupted, Doris' education was further punctuated by her responsibilities as a Prefect. In that capacity, one of her jobs was to supervise the collecting of school scrap.

'We hardly went to school really, but when we did, instead of sitting down to learn something, I spent most of my time out in the corridor sorting out bottle tops and other bits of metal. There were loads and loads of them, and it was my job to sort them and gather them all up. Then somebody else came and took them all away. We always seemed to be collecting.'

One of the big wartime campaigns was "Saucepans for Spitfires" with people encouraged to donate their aluminium pans for smelting. In the event, this reclaimed metal was not used not for aircraft, but for munitions and components.

At fourteen, Doris left school and started work. Her route to work was along an alley at the rear of a row of houses.

'I was taken on as an apprentice bookbinder and was set to learn the trade. I used to go home for lunch as it was quite near my home and one day on the way back to work, I got caught up in a dog-fight. I was crouched at the back of the houses and the planes were machine gunning. Things started to fall around me at my feet. I remember picking one up and it was hot. Eventually, I got back to work and I remember I couldn't speak. I was so traumatised.'

Despite such events, she and her family survived the war intact. Others were not so lucky. A former worker at the printers where Doris worked had joined the Land Army several months before.

'She lived in Henty Road, Worthing. Her house was bombed and her mother was killed. I remember it and it was very sad. She came to see us and it was very hard to know what to say.'

After the war Doris became a Tiller Girl and travelled the world. She now lives in Sussex.

CHAPTER FOURTEEN

Elsie Burberry - Child - Bullet Maker

When she was six years old, Elsie Burberry from South Godstone in Surrey spent much of her time at her grandmother's house. Her aunt, who worked in the munitions factory at nearby Bletchingly, also lived there.

One morning, Elsie came down to breakfast to find an interesting addition to the usual paraphernalia on the kitchen table.

'There was a block of wood screwed to the table and it had a metal spike about six inches long sticking up from it, with a metal dome on top of that.'

It was a device for making aircraft shells, a job with which Elsie soon became acquainted.

'My aunt had brought it home from the factory and fixed it onto the table so that Gran could make bullets at home. But because I was there a lot of the time, I was roped into help as well.'

The factory operated on piece work, with workers paid according to the number of bullets they made. The demand for ammunition was high but with the disruption caused by air-raids, time in the shelters meant less pay. So women took the components home and made up the shortfall there.

'We had a big box of paper cases. They were like cylinders and you had to slide them over the dome, plait the end over and then glue it. I think the paper cases were the bits that held the explosives'.

Even at the age of six, Elsie took her turn in the process.

'It was my job to hold the case up to the light and check there were no holes in it. Once I'd done that, Gran or my aunt used to use a waxed rag and wipe the cylinder so that it fitted properly inside the case. We used to sit and talk while we were doing this. We never had any money or anything and so we stayed in. That's just what people did in those days, and it was just Gran's way of earning a bit of money I suppose - and doing a bit for the war effort.'

Even though there was a munitions factory nearby, Elsie has no memories of being afraid.

'I don't remember being scared in the early part of the war although we were bombed. It was quite ironic that children (evacuees) were coming down to spend time in the village to get away from all the bombs in the big towns and we'd get the stray planes who'd drop their bombs on their way to London or on the way back. It was quite exciting really, not scary.'

One or two incidents in particular stuck in her young mind.

'We had a couple of bombs that dropped on the village but they didn't explode, and we did have a lot of incendiaries. Once, a landmine damaged the school. I remember Dad was at the bottom of the stairs and he called me to come down quickly and I did - the blast of one of them blew me down - but luckily for me I had a soft landing because he caught me.'

Sometimes, the danger came from people on their own side.

'We lived in the High Street next door but one to a petrol garage. The Canadian soldiers that were billeted across the road used to have jerry cans and they'd fill them up with petrol but they never used to switch the pump off. The petrol used to spill and run all over the ground and you can imagine how dangerous that was. We were lucky we didn't get blown up with somebody smoking near the spilled stuff.'

As Elsie got older, she began to understand more about what was happening.

'I don't think I really worried much about the war in the early days. I do remember watching dog-fights though and on one occasion seeing a German plane shooting at a parachutist as he came down. The plane went round and round and machine-gunned him. That wasn't very nice and I remember my mother was really swearing at them for doing that.'

Then, everything changed.

'When I was eleven, we started to get the doodlebugs. That was a bit hairy and I didn't like that at all. I remember seeing the glow of the fires in London. It was twenty miles away but we could still see them from the village. My mother had my brother by then and, as she was Welsh, we went down to Wales to stay with my other grandmother and get away from it.

Perhaps Elsie was too young to be really influenced by the events going on around her, but a chance meeting made her realise that the enemy, in many ways, was not so different from her own family.

'When I was leaving school, just after the end of the war, a teacher invited me to play with her two children. She had two German students there. They were a bit older than I was but they were so nice, pleasant, and I was really pleased to meet them. I think that made me see that they were just the same as us and they didn't want to be involved - it was only Hitler. Their dads had had to go and fight just like ours.

Elsie now lives in Sussex.

THE ARMED SERVICES

Events of the Second World War transformed Britain irrevocably. Many volunteered at the start but when the National Service Act was passed in 1941 women, for the first time, were called up.

Some remained civilians working towards the war effort; others enlisted in one of his Majesty's Armed Services.

Following their induction, they were then despatched to their various units, sometimes with a modicum of choice for the type of work on offer, but more often without it.

They served in all support roles, and later went overseas to support the men at the front line.

After the surrender in Europe, they supervised war reparation and the collection of German ordnance.

Nearly half a million women served in the Armed Services during the war and, of those enlisted, over six hundred were killed on active service.

CHAPTER FIFTEEN

Isabel Eakins - Timber Corps/ATS

One of the great benefits of the Second World War was its socialising effect. As men and women from different backgrounds worked alongside each other, they became united by a common fear: defeat.

Isabel Eakins was one of three sisters from Suffolk. Her father had died shortly before war started.

'The house was a great, big old house but we were as poor as church mice. Mother worked as a secretary in Ipswich, and we also had Granny living with us. I was eighteen and a half when the war started and until then had lived at home.'

It was Isabel's younger sister who first mooted the idea of doing war work. She joined the Land Army and went to a chicken farm not far from home.

'I decided that I should do something as well but, whilst I didn't mind working on the land, I didn't want to farm - but I quite fancied trees. So I asked the woman in the Land Army recruiting place if I could do something with them. I was a bonny girl and I knew that I could swing an axe and she suggested a division of the Land Army, The Women's Timber Corps.'

Being a Suffolk girl, Isabel was sent to Culford St Mary Forestry Camp, one of the biggest in Britain. The arrangement suited her well. She was doing work that she liked and was still near enough home to make leave periods worth looking forward to.

As many services, particularly gas and electricity, had been disrupted or destroyed by bombing, wood was a viable fuel source. It was also a valuable raw material suitable for building aircraft frames, air-raid shelters and repairing bomb damage. The Timber Corps ensured the supply met the demand.

'We women cut the trees down and sawed them up into lengths that the men then dragged away. Some of the girls did that bit as well and also worked in the saw mills, but I worked in the chopping down department.'

For most Timber Corps women, the felling of a tree was a new experience.

'These trees were great big things. Firstly you have an axe and you cut what they call a 'fell' in the side of the trunk. That's like a sideways 'v' shape. Then you kneel down and start to cut through the tree trunk with a bow saw - one woman at each end. Then, when you hear it start to go, you push it forward and it comes down. Then you have to dig a pit about three feet deep, lop the top of the tree off as well as all the rubbish - that all goes in the pit - and then you burn it. We women did all of this - all by hand, all day long. It was a good life but very hard work.'

Although the men took the wood to the sawmills, it was the women who chopped the felled timber into the required lengths.

'We used to measure the tree and cut it into segments

depending on what was needed. We had axes, billy-hooks and saws and we cut the wood up and manhandled it into piles.'

It was at this time that Isabel earned promotion.

'I was promoted to pit prop measurer. I had to mark the trunk into certain lengths and tell the girls what to cut. I was well-paid for doing that job. I got thirteen and six!'

Pit props were used in both mines and for air-aid shelter construction.

'Some shelters were just trenches with earth thrown up over them and piled up at the sides, with the tops covered by branches and soil. Our pit props were used as the sides, but we also cut them for the mines so they could still get coal for the munitions factories.'

For eight and a half months, Isabel felled and chopped, living with thirty-five other women in a hut. Their day began at five and finished in the early afternoon. The only way to get to work was to walk. Come the end of the day that walk seemed twice as long.

'It was a very long day, physically. We didn't have bicycles, just our feet. In between, we chopped and sawed and dragged and dug. It was hard work but I enjoyed it.'

The women came from diverse backgrounds. Tough women from the northern mills, women from the cities who had never been to the country before and, women like Isabel who, had the war never happened, would have been unlikely to have done manual work. Yet, despite their differences and the arguments that would occasionally break out, a strong bond developed between them.

'There were all sorts. Some were very rough, some had muscles like iron and some didn't like washing their necks.

Then there were those who stole - they'd pinch your clothes. But even so, they were good girls and they worked very hard. And they'd look after you; they'd give you a Player's Weights any time!'

After the months in the forestry camp, Isabel's life had changed considerably. Now clad habitually in working clothes, her mother, although proud that her daughter was engaged in useful war work, was driven to voice her disappointment.

'I remember her saying to me once: "Darling, what have you got on? Those awful dungarees." She didn't like me wearing trousers - she was a bit of a snob, really.'

Although she loved the outdoor life, it soon began to pall, and she considered leaving the Timber Corps. When her friend Daphne decided to join the WRNS, Isabel decided that she, too, would follow suit and move on.

'Daphne's father was a doctor and she had no trouble getting into the WRNS. But when I went along, I spoke to this rather snooty recruiting officer who asked me if my father was an Admiral. When I said "no", she asked me what connection I had with the Navy. Well, I had none and that clearly wasn't what she wanted to hear, so she told me to go down the corridor to the ATS office and try there. She passed the buck about me joining up!'

Fortunately, the Army was more realistic. Once in possession of her uniform, she was sent to Fenham Barracks in Newcastle for basic training.

'I can still see the long table where the uniform was laid out; trousers, socks, hat, shoes and a big kit bag. It all got shoved into that. My mother was horrified once again. "You're not going to wear another uniform are you?" It was all so different for her.'

Her arrival at Fenham coincided with a visit from the Luftwaffe. Just as she got to the camp gates an air-raid started.

'This man shouted: "Oi, you can't walk across the parade ground, love. Come in here." So I went into his hut and was given a big mug of tea and a doughnut and I remember thinking: "Oh my God - look at me with this sticky bun!"

Eventually, she made it into the camp and was billeted in a Nissan hut with fifteen other women. The beds were basic: two blankets, a pillow and no linen.

'I remember crying myself to sleep that night. I had no sheets and it really brought it home to me: What had I done?'

If she found the sleeping arrangements rough, Isabel was soon to discover that life in the Army was very different from anything so far experienced. Basic training was about discipline - and being shouted at.

'We had this really mean staff sergeant. He had piercing blue eyes and a waxed-end moustache, hat over his eyes, ribbons on his chest from the First World War, and he'd come right up to you and shout. He nearly marched us to death. Up and down and round and round, saluting and the like. Then he'd send us up to the top floor of the barracks - there were about six floors - and tell us to get our great coats and a gas mask and then he'd make us march round and round again.'

Not surprisingly, Isabel took a deep dislike to him.

'I really didn't like his attitude towards women. One day, he came up and stared at me and shouted: "Stick your chest out!" I said: "I am, that's the lot." He didn't like that at all and he said: "Do you know what a fizzer is?" I said: "Yes, it's a drink of lemonade." This made him really cross and he said: "Right, you're going on a fizzer for being rude. Now, answer me again. Stick your chest out." I said: "Yes, sergeant!" A fizzer was a punishment. Forty-eight hours in a room on your own, no talking. It was a discipline thing.'

By the end of thirteen weeks of square bashing, Private Eakins thought she was ready for anything.

'We had a big passing out parade with a full Scots band. And as I marched past that man, he winked at me. Later, he wrote in my autograph book: "Private Isabel Eakins you will go far because you've got guts." I was really touched by that, especially after the way he'd treated us. And when we were leaving, he came and shook us all warmly by the hand and he said to me: "Good luck. You're a smashing woman, you'll go far." And all because I'd hated him and stood up to him!'

When she had joined up, Isabel had two ambitions. She wanted to drive and to train as a nurse. As a fully-fledged soldier, she now had ample opportunity for both. Sent to Southern Command ATS, she began driving duties on utility trucks, transporting small goods around the South East. As the driver, she was also responsible for the daily servicing of her vehicle.

'We did the cleaning and the greasing, oiling with the grease guns down the pit, cleaned the engines and that. Anything more and it went into the workshops.'

From there, she graduated to staff driving.

'The utilities were dead easy to drive and you used to get daily jobs taking butter and guns and that from camp to camp. But then I got a bit fed up so I asked my friend Jock if I could drive officers. He told me to apply to Colonel Smith from the Dental Corps who needed a driver. So I did and I began to drive him about.'

With the change of cargo, came a change of vehicle.

'His staff car was a Humber Super Snipe, a beautiful car to drive. So smooth. Later on, I was Dame Mary Thyritt's driver. She was the senior commander of the FANY's.'

By the time Isabel joined the ATS, the FANY's - the First Aid Nursing Yeomanry - had amalgamated with the ATS as part of the Royal Army Service Corps, providing drivers for most Army support work.

Another of Isabel's regular jobs was to take supplies to Tilbury docks - in a three-ton Bedford lorry. Tilbury was just one of the ports where hospital ships docked, bringing home the wounded. Shortly after she began those assignments, she asked for a first-aid course.

'They trained me and then put me on Austin KT's - ambulances. They were my forté. I loved driving them. They had four stretchers in the back and we used to collect wounded men. That was very sad. I used to go to Tilbury and Dover or Folkestone to the hospital ships and take wounded men back to the hospital in Maidstone, Ashford or to Leeds Castle where there was a big burns unit.'

She also drove the wounded to hospital after a V1 attack on her own base in Harrietsham, just south of Maidstone.

'We had a lot killed there and I drove them to Maidstone and Ashford. A doodlebug had landed on the

Sergeants' Mess.'

The ambulance crews were all women. They lifted, loaded and unloaded wounded men and kept them comfortable on the way to hospital. They frequently had to improvise to keep the patients calm.

'I remember going to Dover once and picking up this chap who was a double amputee. As we carried him down the gangplank and put him into the back of the ambulance, he said to me: "Oi, Miss, I've lost me leg." He'd actually lost both but we couldn't tell him that, so I said to him: "No, you're ok, here's your leg, feel it." And I quickly rolled up some blankets into tubes, put them where his legs used to be, wrapped him in a blanket, strapped it round him and sent him off. Poor chap. I think he lived, but I don't know what happened to him.'

The burns unit at Leeds Castle provided similar experiences.

'There were a lot of pilots at Leeds, badly burned. I was wandering among them one day and there was a man a completely swathed in bandages. This chap had been flying Spitfires and he called me over. He had a letter in his hand and he asked me to read it to him. Well, it was from his fiancée and it said: "I can't remain engaged to you as you're in such a mess" and that she was ending it. It was terribly sad and I remember him crying through his bandages. I felt it a bit then, when I saw all the burns, but that was how it was.'

However, there were lighter moments.

'When I'd been in the Timber Corps, we'd had to go out hedging. We got taken into the country and dropped here and there by Army truck. One of the drivers was called

Ginger and I didn't like him - he was a cocky little devil, and he'd always pat my bottom as I clambered back into the truck. Anyway, he called me 'Bubbles' and, on this day, I'd gone to Folkestone to meet the wounded off the boat and I said: "Right, we'll take this one." As I went to lift up this chap who was very badly wounded, he said: "I know that voice, it's 'Bubbles'! It was Ginger! I was absolutely stunned! He'd been a despatch rider and he'd been blown off his bike. He was very badly wounded. But he lived.'

The camaraderie of war meant that colleagues helped each other out. For some, like Isabel, whose job entailed daily association with the dying and the badly wounded, a little bending of the rules helped a great deal.

'Sometimes, the sergeant who dished out the jobs would give us a chitty for a made-up job. That meant we could use a truck or a car to go to Maidstone in an evening to have something to eat or to go to the pictures. It was a way of helping take our minds off things I suppose.'

It was after one of these spurious assignments that Isabel made a startling discovery.

'I had a rather nice leather jerkin and, after a few hours, I realised I'd left it in the lorry, so I went to get it. Although the FANY's and the ATS had combined, some of the FANY girls were a bit snooty and you could tell that they really didn't like being part of the common Army. There was one called Audrey who was particularly aloof. I remember she had very red hair and we used to call her 'ginger knob', and that she'd never speak to us. Anyway, as I rolled up the shutter of the lorry, I became aware of something in the back on the floor. It was Audrey - having it off with an officer. She was very embarrassed as you'd imagine, but she was always very nice to me after that!'

As part of Southern Command, Isabel spent her war in one of the most active parts of the country. This offered some interesting additions to her general driving duties. For a while, she was staff driver to Colonel Chinn, part of a unit responsible for secret agents working in the field.

'Quite often I'd drive him to Dover Castle and we'd have a big basket of pigeons. We'd have to take them to the top of the castle, right up on one of the towers, and release them. They all had rings with messages attached and we'd launch them into the air, sending them off to France. You had to hold them in your hands and gently swing them left, then right, then to the middle and then let go. This was to let them judge the air and get a bearing on their surroundings.'

Later the same day, Isabel and Colonel Chinn would go back to the launch tower and retrieve any birds that had returned.

'We'd usually let about twenty birds go but not that many would come back. Some would be wounded, with bits of wing missing. Colonel Chinn would take any messages off them and we'd take the birds back down into the castle.'

She also spent some time underground at Dover Castle, working on communications for secret operations.

'That was a very strange time. There are passages and tunnels under the castle and we'd be down there, only twenty or so miles away from the Germans and we'd work mostly at night. It was weird but I suppose, looking back on it, night was the safest time for the agents behind the lines to be out and about.'

Isabel never got a posting abroad. Her recent marriage

meant that she had to stay in England.

'It was very annoying, very inconvenient. But then I became pregnant and had to leave anyway, so that was the end of my war. I went out - 'paragraph nine.' The Army had paragraphs for everything. If you died, you were out - 'Death: paragraph one.' If you got pregnant you were out: 'paragraph nine.' I can't remember what two to eight stood for.'

After her son was born, Isabel returned to Suffolk and spent the rest of the war with her mother. Nearly sixty years later, like many of her contemporaries, she recalls her war years favourably.

'We all mucked in together and that helped us all deal with things like the constant loss of life, but people stood by you. You had such a busy day that you didn't really have time to think about it. It taught me discipline, though, and when I look back, I can't imagine what it would have been like had I stayed with my mother in the big house. Mind you, she worked all through the war and had a doodlebug come down in a tree in the garden!'

After the war Isabel Eakins worked with the Red Cross. She now lives in Surrey.

CHAPTER SIXTEEN

Muriel Poole - ATS

On being bombed out for the third time, Muriel Poole decided that enough was enough. It was time for her to get her own back.

'We lived in Woolwich, just down from the barracks, and I suppose there were two big reasons for them to have a go at us. There were the munitions works at Woolwich Arsenal and then the barracks. We lived right in the middle.'

On her first encounter with a bomb, the house next door in Samuel Street took a direct hit. Muriel and her family were in the air-raid shelter.

'The rubble and the debris buried us down there but because people knew where we were, they came and got us out. The next time it was just blast - you got used to that, having no windows and no ceilings and that. That was quite normal.'

The episode that still sticks in her mind was when her flat in Francis Street, was hit.

'We lived in a flat above the Post Office and I wouldn't have believed it unless I'd seen it with my own eyes. The blast had ripped the front door off and at the same time lifted up the hall stand, then deposited the door under it, before dropping the hall stand back down again on top of it. So there we were, no door, no windows and open to the world as it were!'

The damage was caused by a landmine, and that was the turning point for Muriel.

'After the hallstand incident, Mum and Dad moved up the road to Charlton and stayed out the war there, although they got blasted again. But I decided I needed to hit back.'

In the early days and, as a married woman, Muriel would not have been called up for war work, but she volunteered anyway. Initially, she worked in a munitions factory in the north of England at RAF Blackburn. This was convenient, as her husband was stationed nearby. It had its drawbacks but, financially, she did quite well.

'It was all piece work and the foreman was from Woolwich Arsenal, so being from Woolwich myself, he gave me all the plum jobs, but it was dreadful. I hated it. I'd never come across anything like it. There were some really nasty characters working in that factory and it was awful.'

Nevertheless, she bore it for three months. When her husband was posted to the south coast, Muriel followed. On a weekend in London, she decided to transfer her talents to the Army. The authorities had other ideas.

'I went to the Labour Exchange but they said, "Oh no, you're on a job of National importance, you'll have to go back." But I wasn't going to, so I refused. We argued and argued and I went back and forth to the Labour Exchange, telling them that I wanted to join up and them telling me

I'd go to prison if I didn't go back to my job of National importance. Three months this went on - they wasted all that time fussing and in that time I was doing no work.'

Eventually, persistence paid off and Muriel won the argument. In early 1942 she joined the ATS.

'I was sent to Edinburgh for my basic training. They taught us things like how to wear a uniform and salute, how to walk properly and how not to disgrace the uniform - all really useful stuff. But I did enjoy being there because I felt I was actually doing something.'

However, Muriel's military career got off to a shaky start.

'At the end of training, we had a weekend leave and I went to see my husband in Hull. Well, I missed the train and, by the time I got back to Edinburgh the rest of my intake had gone, all posted. So I had to stay and wait for the next lot to pass out. I was put to work with the Medical Officer. I really hated that but I suppose I realised that it was just another adventure and I got on with it.'

From Edinburgh, she went to Aldershot to train as a height finder, ready for work on an ack-ack gun battery. From there she went to firing camp at Whitby in North Yorkshire.

'Our gun site was up a hundred and ninety-nine steps and it was right next to a graveyard. It was quite an adventure going up there every day.'

'Predictors and height finders used these long scope things - tubes with a screen at each with an image of an aeroplane on each. You moved it and adjusted it so that both images were right and matched. Then you'd shout

"Height finder on target!" and the girl on predictors would shout "Predictor on target!" and then the command would be given for the firing crew to fire the gun.'

Not long into the war, Muriel lost a colleague and friend.

'I was at Woolwich Common and our offsite was Hilly Fields in Brockley. We got a direct hit there. One of the girls was killed and that was really sad. But it was the only time we lost somebody close.'

Gun crews went to firing camp fairly regularly. The purpose was to give them practise in new techniques, keep them up-to-date with developments in equipment, and brush-up on their aircraft recognition skills. It was also an opportunity for fun - and a break from the constant stress of their work.

'We used to go to Anglesey; that was a good camp. It was wonderful; we used to swim in the sea everyday. I liked the climate up there. It was lovely.'

On her return to Woolwich, Muriel was promoted and requested a move.

'I didn't want to do anything wrong or be put in a position where people might expect me to turn a blind eye. So I thought it was best to move on, although it meant starting out again. But it worked out well and I had a very nice officer in charge.'

Her new posting was Dartford in Kent, with the offsite on Crayford Golf Course.

'Before the war it had been carefully tended and landscaped. All those heavy guns and lorries didn't do it much good, but we weren't there to play games, we had a job to do.'

When the bombing raids died down after the Blitz , a

period of frustration set in for the ack-ack crews. By now highly experienced and well-trained, the men and women of the gun batteries around London had to sit back and watch as the V1 flying bombs arrived.

'We weren't allowed to fire on those because of the danger of bringing them down on residential areas. We had to just let them go through and hope that people got out of the way.'

However, there was no such frustration at the coastal batteries of Kent and East Sussex.

'I was moved down there after the Blitz and we could shoot at them, then. There was nothing apart from marshes there, so there was no danger to towns.'

With the Allies gradually gaining control, gun crews were sent to continental Europe. Muriel, by now a company sergeant major, volunteered for an overseas posting and was sent to Southampton to join a troop ship. From there they sailed to Dover, to await an escort through the minefields in the Channel. This journey was to produce their greatest casualties.

'Everybody on board was violently sick because it was so rough. It was terrible. That was worse than the danger of getting blown up by the mines. But we eventually got to Ostend, where we had to wait for the Battle of the Falaise Gap to finish. Depending on who won, we would either stay and do what we'd come to do, or have to get back on that boat and cross the water again. And none of us wanted to do that!'

Fortunately for Muriel and the other gunners, the Allies were victorious and her battery took over from a marine emplacement near Antwerp.

'None of the men were A1 physically fit. If they had been they'd have been up at the front line. Many had been out in Malaya and Burma, and had been injured. They thought it was very degrading to be sent to a mixed Battery. It was the worst thing that could happen to them. But they soon changed their tune. They lived the life of Riley.'

When the hostilities in Europe finished, her company was sent to an airfield where they collected in heavy machinery from all over Europe.

'It certainly was a big adventure but I don't remember being scared as such. You were so busy doing what you had to do that you didn't really think about yourself. I did used to worry about my husband, though. He was in North Africa and I didn't see him for three and a half years. We wrote regularly but I did worry that he was all right.'

Muriel resumed married life after the war and worked for the Post office. She now lives in Hastings - and like all old soldiers she remembers her Army number.

'Poole, Company Sergeant Major, W 135608. And that's something I've remembered over the years and don't need to look up - I can't remember my own phone number sometimes but I do know my Army number!'

CHAPTER SEVENTEEN

Peggy Steel- ATS

As well as offering new opportunities, the Second World War had a great levelling effect. Nobody was safe, and the feeling of mortality cut right across social barriers, impenetrable for years.

Peggy Steel from Leyton was one of a family of seven. In 1939 she was sixteen and working in a mica factory. The company manufactured parts for aircraft and small electrical items. After two years she decided to move on and, with two friends, applied to join the Women's Auxiliary Air Force (WAAF). Unfortunately, her application was mislaid.

'I'd hoped that us three could stay together but I never did find out what happened to my forms. They got in and I was left behind.'

A year later, Peggy tried again and was accepted by the ATS.

Her new job was Command Post telephonist, Royal Artillery, on a heavy ack-ack gun site between Newport and Cardiff.

'I'd never been to Wales before, so that was an experience. I also did a couple of stints in Anglesey at firing camp, and then down at Bude in Cornwall. I found it very interesting and I loved going to different parts of the country.'

Her 'office' was unusual.

'My job was to operate the wireless and the telephones. We were in a bunker under the actual guns and we worked shifts - a twenty-four hour stint and the next night off.'

'Some of the girls were on predictors - that was finding the height and speed of approaching aircraft. It was quite specialised and, without them, the guns would have been useless.'

By 1943, Hitler's bid for air supremacy had failed. With the RAF still a force to be reckoned with, his attention turned elsewhere. Eventually, in 1944, the ack-ack section was disbanded.

'We never got to fire our guns in anger - the Germans had been and gone by the time I got there. The big raids were over but we still had to be ready in case they returned.'

Peggy was reassigned. She went to London, to a branch of the Royal Army Pay Corps.

'We had to make up pay and do all the records. It was all paperwork then, working in an office, same as in peace time.'

Ironically, it was while she was involved in such ordinary tasks that she experienced the intrusive effects of war as an enlisted woman.

'It was during the time of the V1's - the doodlebugs. I was working in central London, billeted in a very nice house in Mayfair. One day, we were on the bus to Victoria and all of a sudden the driver yelled: "Duck!" and we all did. Mind you, I don't know what good that would have done! But we all escaped injury.'

Although the incident frightened her, the Blitz had been far more terrifying.

'I'd seen far worse before I'd joined up. We'd had the Blitz and all the raids on London, on the docks. That was a very frightening time. Down the shelter every night until morning, then back off to work. Three of my sisters had been evacuated but they weren't happy and Mum wasn't happy with them being away. Dad had died before the war and she'd worked so hard to keep us seven kids together. I think she thought they were safer with her.'

Shortly after the incident on the bus, Peggy was allowed to live at home.

'The authorities decided that anybody who lived within a certain radius could live in their own house if they wanted to. Maybe they thought if we were going to get killed, we might as well get killed in cheaper places than Mayfair! So I went back to Leyton and travelled to work every day, like an ordinary office worker. Mind you, we did get bombed and shot at, so it wasn't quite the same.'

The utilitarian style of their clothing was, according to Peggy, a source of wry amusement. Clad habitually in battle dress, boots and, trousers, music reflected her life back then.

'One night we were walking along and there was a moon. Somebody said, "Look at us," and started to sing that song, "Moonlight Becomes You." And there was another song we had - "So Tired." It became our theme tune because we were - we were always so tired.

After the war, Peggy retrained and became a machine operator with the National Cash Register Company.

CHAPTER EIGHTEEN

Mildred Veal - ATS

By 1943, it was commonplace to find women doing men's jobs. Many taboos had evaporated in the slipstream of necessity. But what happened when there was an occasional lull in the storm over British skies, and that coveted bit of downtime when the guard, albeit never dropped, enjoyed a brief respite? Many women just resumed women's work - even on the gun sites.

By the time Christmas Day dawned that year, Britain had been at war for over four years. Twenty-one year old Sergeant Mildred Veal was hoping for a restful day. Although it seemed that the Germans had decided to stay at home, there was still plenty to do - looking after the men. While women did men's work, men rarely returned the compliment.

'It seemed I was tired most of the time. We all were. It was just one of those things. And how I'd have loved a bit of a lie-in as a present that day - it was Christmas. But the men were there, so that was that!'

Mildred and the other women were up at dawn.

'We made buckets of tea so the men could enjoy a Christmas cuppa in bed. Then it was off to the cookhouse to start the breakfast. Eggs, bacon, fried bread, and more tea - for fifty. After that, there was just time to wash up the greasy pots in buckets of cold water, before I had to play the piano for the Christmas sing-song. I can't remember when we had our breakfast, or even a cup of tea, but I'm sure we did. Mind you, we had to do it for ourselves. Only the men got waited on.'

With the singing over, it was time to peel the potatoes for Christmas dinner.

'I can remember the Christmas noises and the cosy atmosphere in the Mess. But we were out in the cookhouse again, peeling spuds, hundreds of them. They seemed to go on forever!'

Once lunch was underway, the tables had to be laid and bottles of beer put out.

'We didn't have much by today's standards but we seemed to make what we did have go a long way. And we were rushed off our feet.'

Then it was time. The time they'd all been waiting for. Christmas dinner on the table and delicious smells wafting out into the cold bright day. For a few minutes the roar of excitement and anticipation dimmed as the seated men savoured those first mouthfuls of food, served by the ever-attendant women. Merriment and delight blended with familiarity, as the ritual of Christmas mixed battledress and party hats into an elixir of normality.

'Then the bloody alarm bell went off and everybody ran for the guns. Two hours we were all out there, and with the dinner on the table going cold. Typical. How I cursed the Germans then!'

As if to add insult to injury, it was only a lone bomber,

circling, just out of range, laughing down at the group in party hats. Far worse, a train full of service men parked on an adjacent railway line, were delighted by the gunners' wrath.

'They thought it was highly amusing - all these girls running around trying to get that one bloody plane. And we knew our dinner was getting cold! '

Eventually, the German went home, the train moved on, and the gunners became revellers once more.

'When we got back in, the food had to be warmed up. The men were in the Mess and we were out the back working like mad things to get it back on the table and guess what? The generator caught fire! Well, I don't know how we sorted it out, but we did, and in the end everybody got fed.'

With full stomachs, the men snoozed comfortably in the warm atmosphere while Mildred and the others cleared away. Then it was time for tea, more clearing up and Mildred went back to her post at the piano.

'I can remember falling into bed, exhausted. Even if the Germans had come back that night, I wouldn't have heard 'em. I was done in. That was my Christmas Day 1943. So much for a rest! '

Mildred Veal had not intended to join the Army. Her first choice had been the Women's Auxiliary Air Force, an ambition guided more by vanity than ambition.

'I liked their hats. It was as simple as that. The hats were lovely and I quite fancied wearing their uniform. But it turned out that my eyesight wasn't good enough, and I ended up as a gunner instead '

In early 1941, Mildred, now enrolled in the ATS, went to

Neville's Cross Barracks in Durham for a month of square-bashing. From there she was posted to Brigstock near Kettering, as a clerk to the Quartermaster's Stores in a searchlight battery. When she volunteered for ack-ack work, she moved again, this time to Oswestry in Shropshire.

'I went on Boxing Day and it was bitterly cold I remember. Then I went back down to London where I was based at a battery in Barking Park, Essex. All these houses backed onto the park and I remember wondering if it was worse for the people to be disturbed by the noise of the guns or the noise of the bombs.'

Years later, she found out from a former local resident: Dame Vera Lynn. The singer told Mildred that although both were frightening, the uncertainty of what might happen was even worse. When Mildred discovered just whom she had been keeping awake, she revelled in the irony.

'To think we used to listen to Vera Lynn on the wireless and sing her songs to keep us going! With all that din, it's a wonder she remembered her words!'

For a woman with poor eyesight, Mildred's Army career progressed quickly. Promoted to corporal in March 1942, then to lance sergeant in July of that year, she proved herself more than capable. By the end of the year, she was a full war substantive sergeant.

'FWSS is when you get your gun. My job was to run the team that took the telephoned warnings that came from the Royal Observer Corps people, and find the enemy on the Radar screen. We tracked the planes as they came into our sector. Once we'd got them, I'd give the order to the command post for the gun crew. The women there would find the height and predict the range and speed of aircraft to get the guns on target to shoot them down.'

Mildred ran a team of twenty-three women at her Radar station, working in four groups of six. The Germans had no idea that the British had developed Radar and were using it to intercept their aircraft.

'It was highly secret. We had no officers up there at all and only we women were allowed in. We could pinpoint the exact position of enemy aircraft and the early warning meant that the gun crews had the opportunity to decide on what fuse they needed, and the angle to take account of their height and speed. The shell has to go up in front of an aircraft for it to have any effect and Radar meant that they could fire them where they were needed.'

Mildred then went down to Plymouth to do the same job for a year, before returning to London for the V1s and V2s. The secrecy of the posting meant that the women also had to service their own machinery.

'We had this fifteen-kilovolt generator and one day the sump needed to be cleaned out. I decided to do it and so I got under it with a bucket and a mop. But I forgot that I'd taken a bolt out; the whole contents of the sump emptied out over my head. They always said that you could tell a gun layer waller by the stink of diesel and grease. Well, you certainly could with me on that day!'

Just after the end of the war, Mildred was promoted to staff sergeant before being 'relegated to the unemployed list' in January 1946. She retained her reserve status until the mid 1950's, transferring to the WRAF before eventually becoming a civilian once again.

By the end of her military service, she had achieved the rank of captain, was a fully qualified fighter controller and entitled, at long last, to wear her first choice of hat.

Mildred now lives in York. She still plays the piano and is one of the trustees to the fund for the Memorial to the Women of World War Two.

CHAPTER NINETEEN

Jane Pope - Ciphers

Jane Pope from Greenock was nearly twenty-one when the war started. An articled clerk to a firm of accountants, she still had eighteen months to do of her four year commitment - and she hated it.

In early 1939, on seeing the posters asking women to join the Armed Forces, she thought she had found a way out. Her application to become a Wren was accepted, but there was one obstacle she had not bargained for: the principal of her office. When she asked for her articles to be broken, he refused.

'Your father has paid for four years and you'll stay. But if war does break out, we'll let you go.'

With no option but to forget her plans, reluctantly she resumed her office job. However, when war was finally declared, she requested leave to enlist. At first, her boss claimed to have forgotten his promise, but then relented. In December 1939, Jane Pope joined the WRNS.

When she reported to the naval base at Greenock, she told the officer at the enlisting interview that she wanted to be a driver.

'I don't know why I said that; it just came into my head

and it seemed like a good idea at the time.'

Just as all the papers had been completed and she had been given her first orders, she stood to leave. As she did so, a casual last question from the enlisting officer changed the course of her career.

'What are you doing now, Pope?'

'I'm articled at the moment ma'am.'

'Articled for what?'

'For accountancy.'

'Come back here; any fool can drive a car. We need people with good mathematical minds for ciphers and decoding. That's what you'll do.'

Instead of driving her way through the war, Jane Pope signalled instead.

The waters of Western Scotland were home to over five hundred destroyers and corvettes, ships that regularly sailed the Northern Atlantic and beyond. These waters were also infested with a major threat to the home fleet - German U boats.

Cipher and coding was vital work, and Jane was the first woman decoder within this all male environment. Coded signals travelled between the Admiralty and shipping and it was Jane's job to translate them. It required an intellectual ability upon which orders, battle successes and men's safety depended. Many considered it unsuitable work for women.

'The sailors didn't want to know about women. They just looked at me and were generally most unhelpful. I suppose they couldn't be blamed in many ways - they were only ratings, used to women doing women things. They'd never even imagined us beyond the kitchen sink, let alone thought of us as equals before.'

Quietly confident she would not be up to the task, they expected her to fail.

'A signals officer said to me: "There're the books, there's a signal, decipher it; you've got one hour." And he walked out, leaving me to get on with it. Well, I was somewhat bemused but I knew that if I didn't do it, and do it by the time he came back, that would be the end of me and I might have to resume my articles.'

Armed with a pencil, paper and stubborn determination, she got on with it. One hour. One hour to prove she could do her job and make them accept her on her terms.

Perhaps her greatest advantage was her analytical mind and procedural training. Two and a half years of hated accountancy had given her a good grounding. Her father's money had not gone to waste. Pondering over the meaningless marks on the page, Jane finally rested her pencil on the desk just before the officer returned. One hour to the second.

As he picked up the paper he can, perhaps, be forgiven for smiling. The signal was deciphered and deciphered correctly, and within the time limit he had imposed. His smile faded and, without the expected evidence of her ineptitude, he had no option but to take her to the main office where she was to work.

There, signal ratings took plain language signals or message over the telephone and passed them to Jane.

'I never got any help - none at all. I didn't even have a uniform until 1940, so I was different even in that way.'

Her ability became evident very quickly and, before long, four more women were sent to her to train. They were followed by another four and then another, until there were sixteen of them, with Jane overseeing them all. This was the beginning of the cipher school that trained signals operators for the rest of the war.

As the most experienced signaller, it was Jane's job to deal with the odd ones that had defeated others.

'We used to pin them up on the wall and it was my job to deal with them; those that nobody else could do. That was how I spent my days. It would be odd signals in code to be decoded, or signals where the letter groups had been corrupted. The worse ones always seemed to come from submarines.'

After a while, she was sent to Greenock Naval College and commissioned. She then spent three months in London working for Flag Officers (Subs), before being posted to Largs.

'My boss was Flag Officer NOIC - I can't remember what it stands for now, but he was responsible for the armed merchant convoys, especially across the Atlantic. After that, I was shipped off to Northern Ireland to train cipher staff in Belfast. I was working with the Flag Officer Northern Ireland, and it was part of the set-up for CNCWA, which dealt with all the shipping in the Western approaches.'

It was while she was in Northern Ireland that she met her husband, and had their son. Her husband was then sent to Sri Lanka - Ceylon as it was then. The journey did not go well.

'He was torpedoed three times in one year. He left for Ceylon in May but it all kept going wrong. All that time in the water really ruined his health and led to him developing TB. It took him a year to get to the Navy hospital in Ceylon.'

Back in Belfast, Jane received conflicting reports.

'At times I was told he was dead, then missing, then I didn't know, then I found out he was a survivor. It was very hard.'

With a young baby to care for, Jane was given leave, but retained by the WRNS.

'As an officer, you're never really released. I was on indefinite unpaid leave and, eventually, they asked me to go back. I agreed but only with strings. I asked for L & P.A - Lodging and Provisions Allowance. That meant I could rent a place and look after my son. That way, I didn't have to live in and I could keep him with me. I would have had to find somewhere for him otherwise, and I wasn't going to do that.'

Jane found a house, took the Irish nanny with her and moved back to Scotland.

'I did the rest of the war in Glasgow. Then, in 1945, I was sent to the North of Scotland to a Fleet Air Arm base in Invergordon. By the time my husband came home, he'd been away four years. We were both de-mobbed and we went back to Northern Ireland. But his health was no good and he died in 1948.'

Six years of war had taken its toll on Jane

'Towards the end of the war it became very tedious. After about two years of bombing and rations and shortages and, of course, the daily tragedies, we were exhausted. We used to try and do things like dances for the ratings, just to take our minds off things.'

Yet the memories were not all bad.

'I was at a dance that we'd organised for ratings and the CO asked me to dance. He asked me what my name was - we were all known by our surnames - so I said: "My name's Pope, sir". He roared with laughter and asked me again what my name was, so I said: "Pope." He roared again and said: "It can't be, mine's Bishop!" - and it was. It wasn't until he met my mother and I introduced her as Mrs Pope that he finally believed me.'

One of the drawbacks of signals work was understanding the repercussions of battle. The effect, psychologically, was tremendous.

'With deciphering, we always knew what was happening, what ships were lost, how many men were lost, requests for urgent help, that sort of thing. We were dealing daily with loss of life and it was very depressing.'

Accuracy was vital; incorrectly decoded signals could leave a feeling of guilt, even if someone else had made the error.

'I remember one signal that was pinned on the board and left for me. It said: "I have sighted enemy submarine" - then his exact position - and then: "Where am I?" I picked it up during my shift and it troubled me, so I chased it. Then I realised that it had been wrongly decoded. Instead of asking: "Where am I?", it actually said: "Awaiting your instructions." Who knows what happened as a result?'

Occasionally, signals mentioned people Jane knew.

'I remember when I heard about Alex Joy. She was the first Wren in Northern Ireland to volunteer for service overseas and she'd worked with me on ciphers. They were in a convoy en route to Gibraltar. There were about a hundred Wrens on board and the whole lot was lost. That was in mid 1943. I shall never forget it. Alex Joy was such a nice girl.'

After such an eventful war, the privations of its aftermath and the death of her husband, Jane decided to put it all behind her. She moved to South Africa with her small son and lived in Durban until 1995. She now lives in Slovenia.

Private Isabel Eakins

Betty Waters, aged 13

Flo Waters, front right

Joan Crump, Firefighter, 20th August, 1940

Barbara Hooper, Land Girl in Waiting

NFS refresher course, September 1943. Joan Crump, back third from left

Joan Crump with her dog

The Max Sisters, Margaret McFarlane (l) Frances (r)

Margaret McFarlane

Company Sgt Major Muriel Poole

Sgt Mildred Veal

Private Pat Beveridge

Vera Wilson on holiday in Birmingham, June 1944

CHAPTER TWENTY

Pat Beveridge - Intercept Officer

When Pat Beveridge was told she must never reveal what she did during the war, she took it seriously. So seriously, that she kept it from her husband for fifty years.

'A programme came on television about Enigma, and it was only then I realised that was what I had been doing. My husband was very interested in the story, so I thought it was time for me to confess.'

However, when Pat divulged her wartime activities, Hector Beveridge was less than impressed.

'He was most affronted. "I'm your husband" he roared. You're not supposed to keep secrets from me!" Well, they just said not to tell anybody - they didn't make an exception for you dear, I said.'

Pat Beveridge grew up in the North East and had trained as a shorthand typist. When she was twenty-one she was called up to go into the Army. It had never occurred to her that she would have to and, even though her boss arranged a six-month deferrment, in the end, she had no option.

'When I got there, there was an officer who, I now realise was probably quite interesting. But as I didn't want to be in the Army, I really resented her, especially as she told me I must never, ever wear red nail polish. Yet on her nails there it was - red nail varnish. I was terribly affronted. I just didn't understand all this telling people what to do and then doing something completely different yourself.'

On reflection, the officer was clearly more astute than Pat gave her credit for.

'She kept saying to me: "I know what you're going to do", and I said: "I'm going to do secretarial work, I've been trained." She said: "Not on your life." She then told me she knew exactly what I was going to do. And she did.'

After recruitment, the women were given intelligence tests and then ten of the recruits, including Pat, were sent for more.

'It was listening to Morse and we had to mark the correct signal. Well, I didn't like that officer so I marked everything wrongly. I thought, "She's not going to get me away from typing." But by the time it was over, pride had reasserted itself and I'd rubbed all my answers out and written the right ones down.'

After scoring one hundred percent, Pat was sent to London for a series of interviews by a selection of psychologists and officers.

'They were all odd bods and I remember losing my temper with one of them. He asked me what made me think I could do Morse? I shouted at him that I didn't want to do it anyway - it was they who'd said I had to and that I wanted to be a typist. But as he'd asked, I told him I'd already learned one system for words so why wouldn't I be able to learn another?'

Despite her show of resistance, Pat quite liked Morse; it was the Army she loathed. It seems ironic that a woman who admits to being the most unlikely conscript ended up guarding a confidence for over half a century.

'We didn't know what it was all about - well, at least, I didn't. We were in the Army. They just said do this, do that, but nobody ever explained why. So I did.'

From her home in the North East, Pat was sent to Fenham Barracks in Newcastle for basic training.

'It was all a terrible shock to discover that other people whom you considered to be absolute idiots were in charge of you. It was all "Do this, do that." Why? "Don't ask why - just do it!"

For six weeks she endured what she termed 'foot slogging' and learning to respect officers and NCOs.

'You were absolute scum, you were just there. It didn't matter, you were just there to do as they told you.'

Disdainful of military life, she had no recourse but to endure it for the remainder of the war.

'The pay was totally inadequate; just ten shillings a week. By the end of the week, nobody had enough money left for anything. On Friday, we used to put all our change together and buy one doughnut, cut it up and all have a piece.'

Now stationed in Derby at a signals outstation, her work was considered so vital that neither she nor her colleagues had any idea of what they were doing. It was only after the war that she discovered the existence of the three Enigma machines at Bletchley.

'We signed the Official Secrets Act and we were warned that men would stop us at the gates and offer us lifts into Derby, but we were never to tell them anything. So we didn't. I always pretended I was a cook.'

Enigma remained a secret for years; nobody talked about it, and nobody believed that women had been involved in such high security work.

'Years after the war, a friend of my husband's came to dinner. He'd been in signals abroad, and he asked me what I'd done in the Army. So I told him I'd been a Y signals operator and his face absolutely fell. He said: "You couldn't possibly have been. Only men were Y signals operators." I said: "Well, I was." He had been in the Middle East and everywhere and Y signals were terribly important to him. It was a job of prestige and he just couldn't accept that it was women who'd decoded the signals on which he and his men had depended.'

Having learned not to ask questioins, Pat just got on with her work.

'We were intercept officers. I intercepted Morse and wrote it down. Every night at midnight, we were given a new call sign - for example, instead of the ABC that it had been the day before, it was now CAB and you had to turn the dial until you heard somebody sending, saying: "My call sign is CAB." Then you knew you were all right. Then, whatever they sent in Morse, you took down. You didn't change the frequency or anything.'

With Enigma broken, transmissions continued in a format that never changed.

'It was in five letter blocks, in code. As they sent the Morse, we wrote down what we heard. That then went to Bletchley. Apparently, Alan Turin had worked out that if you pushed one key, it came up as another. It all depended on the code for the day, that's why it was important for us to listen for that. But we didn't know why at the time.'

The work captured her imagination.

'I found it interesting and it was a challenge to get the correct message down. But nobody told us anything about where the signals were coming from. We were instructed and that was it. We were at everybody's mercy. However, it became clear from early on to whom we were listening. The length and style of messages gave it away.'

There were also national differences.

'The Italians went berserk. They just went on and on: "Pronto, pronto!" But the Germans were different. A friend of mine had been at school in Germany and she picked up a message one day about how they were bombing Dresden. We learned all sorts of things and it was terrible, just terrible.'

After the fighting in Europe had finished, the Asian war continued.

'When the Germans gave up I thought it would be all over but we quickly had to learn the Japanese system. It was in the same format but another language, another alphabet.'

These signals reminded the women of their own experiences and fears.

'It really hit home to hear them losing friends and family just as we had. It made you wonder just what it was all about.'

But there were also many light sides to Pat's war.

'The Army was a terrible culture shock for me. I'd come from the North East from a background that I thought was perfectly normal and, suddenly, I was amongst all these people who were very strange. It was very funny and very revealing. I learned so much about people's behaviour. It taught me a great deal - particularly never to gossip but it also taught me that I could think for myself.'

Then one day, much to her annoyance, Pat was promoted to corporal. In a burst of defiance, she refused to sew her stripes on, but the women did it for her on the basis that she was as good as any and better than most. But she put her foot down when an officer tried to have her commissioned.

'Commissioned? I didn't want a commission. I didn't even want a corporal's stripe but I could just about manage that. They just wouldn't leave me alone. Why, I don't know. They must have had plenty of people who wanted promotion.'

One day, towards the end of the war, Pat was summoned and told somebody was coming to see her. When he arrived, the man had a black box, fifteen inches wide by two feet long, covered in blue celluloid about four inches wide, arranged in a figure of eight. To this day, she has never heard it mentioned but suspects it was something to do with Colossus, an early computer on trial at the time.

'It was clearly something that worked with something else. When you're taking down Morse there are two types of interference, man made and atmospheric. Sometimes you can't get through it. But with this machine, if you pushed a button it took the message right through. I then had to listen, remove the interference and write the message down.'

It seems she was being used to test run decoding

inventions.

'He explained what he wanted me to do but he never told me why. I had this ticker-tape machine once. I never did find out about that, either. I just find it funny now that men like my husband's friend and so many other people are shocked when they find out that it was we women who helped keep them alive. After all, who did they think tested things? Quite why they should think we didn't have it in us to do it is quite beyond me.'

After the war Pat resumed married life and now lives in West Sussex. She is also a ferocious Bridge player, her mind as sharp as ever.

CHAPTER TWENTY ONE

Joyce Tapsell - ATS

Joyce Tapsell, aged nineteen, was working at the Prudential Assurance Company in Holborn, central London, when war began. From her aunt's home in Finchley, she travelled to work each day on the London and North East Railway. Her mother lived nearby with her other children.

'My aunt never had children of her own and she was a bit older. My uncle was a printer and I had a good life and was well looked after, even though the arrangement may seem a little odd by today's standards.'

But her domestic arrangements changed at the beginning of September. In common with many people, when the actual declaration of war came, it was almost an anti-climax.

'The week before, on the Sunday before the Sunday that war was actually declared, we went to Paddington Station. We'd been warned to pack our bags beforehand and then we were told to report to the station, so we knew it was coming.'

For many months, conflict had been regarded as the likely outcome of the deteriorating relations with Germany. The build-up enabled businesses and organisations to plan evacuation of staff and give them a element of choice.

'They made it so that if you wanted to go with a friend you could arrange to do so but, that weekend, my friend was on holiday. So I had to get in touch with her quickly and tell her to come back. She did. We met at Paddington and went off together.'

The evacuation also gave Joyce freedom.

'It was a chance to break free. I suppose I was being closeted a bit and although my aunt and uncle looked after me well, I wanted to have a bit of my own life.'

From Paddington, Joyce and her friend went to Torquay. Initially, they stayed at a hotel in Babbacombe.

'People were still on holiday when we arrived. It was August and the seaside was a bit tight as far as accommodation went. And then after a while, we got a bit fed up living in hotels, so we moved into a B and B.'

Joyce's job as a shorthand typist involved general office management, and one of her tasks was to type National Insurance cards. The move from London meant that, although she was doing a similar job, she now had a much better view from her 'office' window.

'I carried on doing my typing and stuff but I looked out onto the sea from the hotel. My base was in one of the bedrooms that the Prudential had taken over. It was quite nice really.'

In 1943 and now in her early twenties, Joyce was conscripted into the Army.

'Because I'd been evacuated, I had an exemption from the first wave of conscription. At first I wanted to go into the WRNS but then I chose the ATS because it meant I could travel rather than stay in the area. Devon was very nice, but I didn't come from there and it would have meant staying put. The ATS meant I'd get a chance to move about a bit.'

As a newly enlisted woman, she was sent to training camp at Wrexham in North Wales, before being posted to an ack-ack regiment at Ratho, just outside Edinburgh. Her duties were still clerical.

'I was a shorthand typist, so I worked in the Regimental Office. I typed letters and worked for the CO. It was general office management stuff again, marking up leave cards and making sure that people got paid. And for some reason - I don't know what - my regiment always seemed to be taking over vicarages as Army premises.'

After several months, Joyce asked to be posted south.

'We got forty-eight hour passes but for me to travel all the way from Scotland to London was a waste. So I asked for a transfer.'

She was sent to another ack-ack regiment, this time outside Ashford in Kent. By now, the Germans were using V1 flying bombs. Joyce's regiment had to stop them reaching London.

'Once they'd got that far, they were far more dangerous because they were bombs. If our side did shoot them down, they still caused as much damage because they would then fall onto the houses and buildings below and blow up anyway. So our gunners had to try and stop them before they got that far - if they came down in the countryside, the damage was far less.'

The conditions under which Joyce lived were often rather poor. In Ashford, she lived in a requisitioned house with no bathroom. Fortunately, the local postmistress recognised her plight and allowed Joyce to use hers.

'It was also a bit tricky when we were stationed near Manston because we only had the one ablution - and it was men and women. Eventually, they got things sorted out and we women moved to a better site at Cliftonville, near Margate.'

Joyce certainly fulfilled her wish to travel. As the Regiment moved to deal with the V1 problem, they often moved at short notice. One such move was to Northumberland, by train.

'This was quite interesting as we went by night. We rigged the carriage so we could all lay down - kitbags were the most useful for this but we also used the parcel racks that could be found on old steam trains. We left in such a hurry that we took our cat and her kittens with us. We put them inside our coats and the RSM never knew.'

But if they had had a comfortable journey to Newcastle, their new base fell far short of what they might have hoped for.

'We were billeted in South Shields and I can see it now as we came over the bridge into Newcastle Station to get into the lorries. There was thick snow. It was horrible and we had to melt it for washing purposes.'

One positive aspect of the South Shields camp was that, as a friend of Joyce's came from the area, they were able to go to her home on leave. Her friend's father was also a butcher, giving her the added bonus of fresh meat.

Before long, the Regiment was moved again, this time overseas, but Joyce did not want to go. She applied for another posting.

'They were all going to Belgium and I didn't fancy it. I left the ack-ack regiment and then went to St Leonards near Hastings with the RASC. Our billet there was a modern block of flats on the front nick-named 'the battleship' because of the style. The flats are still there and they're quite posh now.'

Being on the sea front in the bracing air revived an age-old military tradition, come rain or shine: exercise.

'Every morning it was. We had to go down to the promenade for PT. And before breakfast, too.'

After that, she was sent north again, this time to Headingly, just outside Leeds. They had offices on the cricket ground and once again, Joyce was doing clerical work.

'I was a sergeant by that time and I was running an office of women, still managing leave cards and forms and making sure the right people did the right things.'

With the war nearly at an end, she was finally posted back to London, to the War Office in Hobart House. The building overlooked Buckingham Palace and she was billeted in Sloane Square. Eventually, she moved home to Finchley and travelled to work daily.

'We were bombed near home, in Finchley. It was a doodlebug. The sergeant at our base was a real one for the spit and polish. He had this thing outside the door, on display. It was part of the inside of a doodlebug and we had to take it in turns to whitewash it. And that bomb was the end of his display.'

After the war Joyce stayed in the ATS until she married. Her service record shows she was 'relegated to the unemployment list on July 31st due to termination of engagement', with a record of exemplary military conduct.

Like many women from that era, Joyce is grateful for the opportunities the war gave her.

'It was a wonderful experience and we had some great times. I had travelled around, doing a job that I knew, and I'd made some great friends.'

Joyce now lives in Dorking.

CHAPTER TWENTY TWO

Anthea Gregson - WRNS

Glamour and the style of uniform seems to have been a key factor amongst many women who joined up. At twenty-three, Anthea Gregson was already driving an Air Raid Precaution (ARP) ambulance when she decided to enlist.

'I was doing voluntary work with the ARP and I thought that if I joined the WRNS I'd be near civilisation in a port. And, also, it was my favourite uniform.'

Coming from Lancashire and knowing Liverpool well, she expected to be sent there. Instead, she was despatched as a driver to work at the opposite end of the country - the East End of London. But if the uniform was stylish, the accommodation in which they were billeted was definitely not.

'We lived in the most appalling conditions. Bombed out house, no hot water, no windows, boarded up, hardly any furniture. Two double decker bunks and you hung your uniform on the picture rail.'

It was also rather draughty.

'There was a table, but as the door had been blown off its hinges, you had to put the table across the doorway.'

With docks and barracks, Woolwich Arsenal and many

factories concentrated into a small area, the south east and East End of London was a constant target. Consequently, there was little spare or suitable accommodation to house service women. After six months, their health began to deteriorate. They all had permanent colds and even the Admiral in charge of submarines noticed.

'A Wren messenger - I think she was only eighteen this girl - turned round and told him, "If you saw where they lived sir, you'd understand." That very afternoon, he surprised us by inspecting our quarters and sent out a signal, "No hardened seaman would put up with these living conditions ashore."

After the Admiral's intervention, they were moved to more comfortable quarters and their health improved.

Anthea spent two and a half years as a Navy driver in London. She drove many different people including former crowned heads of State and the general in charge of anti-aircraft guns. From her silent position behind the wheel, she overheard many interesting conversations.

'The anti-aircraft General asked our Admiral if the food situation was as bad as he had heard. The Admiral told him that there was only three weeks supply of food left in the country at that particular time. That was probably 1942 and it was due to the submarines doing their worst to our shipping.'

As a staff driver, Anthea also drove officers when they were off-duty. On one occasion, as Admiral Dunbar-Naismith's driver, he told her that later that evening, he would be taking his wife and Lady Mountbatten out. Unfortunately, Anthea had also planned an evening out and this meant that she would now be unable to go.

'My face must have fallen. Six of us had booked tickets for the concert at the Albert Hall with Yehudi Menhuin playing. Well, it turned out that this was where he was going and when he realised, he said, "Well, we'll arrive early and we'll take our time coming out, so don't miss a note of the music." I had a lovely time driving him.'

Then she changed jobs. Now a boarding officer, it was Anthea's responsibility to prepare ships for convoys. The post required great organisation and the ability to think quickly if the need arose. It frequently did.

'On one occasion this captain came into our office one lunchtime, very drunk. We knew he was from a merchant ship but as we had about thirty in the area and we couldn't find out from him which his was, I had to go round all of them until I found it.'

Having arranged for him to be delivered to the correct ship to sleep it off, she returned to her office. The following day, he reappeared.

'He came to apologise and asked if there was anything he could do. As his ship was a loaded collier and the captain of our base had said we could not have the central heating on, I said, "Yes, I'll call about half past five this evening when its getting dark and I'll have a sack of coal, please."

A few months later, after D-Day, Southampton had been virtually taken over by American ships. The American sailors were thrilled to have Wrens as boarding officers.

'I usually had a crew of three girls manning the boats and delivering me to the ships. One sailor brought complete sets of Max Factor makeup for the girls, all the way from America. This was wonderful, as makeup was extremely difficult to get during the war.'

With the ships ready to sail in convoy, those who remained ashore watched with mixed emotions as they departed. On the eve of D-Day a Scottish captain appeared in Anthea's office in search of a large parcel. He had been waiting impatiently for it to arrive from Scotland and this was his last chance to collect it. It arrived later that day.

'It was a set of bagpipes and as his ship up-anchored and sailed for D-Day, he was playing them. "I'll take the High Road." And that was very, very moving.'

Like many women, the war had presented Anthea with an opportunity that she might never otherwise have had. It was an outdoor job, she was not confined to a desk, and she regularly met interesting people. She also had a few surprises.

'One day, a commander asked me to take a Wren to a lunch appointment and bring her back, and to give a young male officer a lift to a train station on the way. So this young chap with fair hair got in the front and the Wren got in the back and, although the chap was chatting away, she never said a word. When we reached the station, he asked if there was a pub nearby. When I said bang opposite, he said, " Right then, I'll stand you girls a drink." And he did.'

Although she had noticed how quiet the other Wren had been, Anthea had no idea why. All she knew was that the young man was a rating, handsome, but a bit too young for her.

'It was Prince Phillip of Greece as he was then. He'd been at some enquiry being held about his ship, The Wallace, but I thought he was just a subbie. I had no idea. But he was very nice, very chatty. The other Wren knew and that's why she'd been tongue-tied. But I had no idea!'

Anthea Gregson now lives in East Sussex and, in keeping with her maritime background, within sight of the sea.

CHAPTER TWENTY THREE

Shirley Pettyfer - Royal Observer Corps

Like many children at boarding school, when the war broke out, Shirley Pettyfer's mother was abroad. The turbulent political situation meant that communication between them ceased almost completely. While Shirley and her sister attended school in England, their next of kin was their mother's sister, Marie, who lived near Bedford.

'I'd finished my exams and it seemed somewhat pointless to stay. So I left without telling anybody. I got the train up to London from Tiverton and then up to Bedford to my aunt's house.'

Her aunt was quite pragmatic about the incident.

'I never even thought that the school might report me missing, but my aunt thought I should tell them just in case. I was expecting trouble but, in the event, nobody seemed very surprised.'

Aunt Marie ran a tea shop in Bedford called 'Barbara's Bun Shop'.

'I helped in the shop for a while but then my aunt said I had to do something for the war effort. So I decided that I would join the Royal Observer Corps.'

The Royal Observer Corps was part of the Air Force. With the country split into regions, aircraft movements were plotted and monitored. Shirley went to Bromham Royal Observer Corps Centre not far from Bedford, the centre for aircraft plotting in the Home Counties.

'I started there in 1944 and we'd work in shifts of eight hours and then we'd get twenty-four hours off. We worked with older men; they were part-time in the Corps and together we plotted what was going on in the skies above our region.'

When the Corps received information about aircraft that were coming their way, the men would plot the numbers, aircraft type and direction. The WAAFs would then move them across a large tabletop map.

'It was tracking. We'd move things around according to the information and pass it on to the relevant gun batteries.

Bromham ROC centre, just outside London, was always busy.

'We were active all of the time and it was a very interesting place to be. I stayed there until D-Day and was there when the Dakotas and gliders went out.'

She also met some interesting people but, looking back, feels she was too young to fully appreciate the significance of all that was happening in Europe.

'We had a lot of Polish and Dutch pilots stationed near to us. The Dutch in particular had come across the sea in little boats and at every opportunity were itching to get back at the Germans. We also had Australians and New Zealanders and I used to try and look after them when some of their friends didn't return. It was quite an extraordinary place to be. Terrible things happened but it was exciting.'

Prototype aircraft were also being developed nearby.

'I didn't realise that the Germans were already testing jets and I suppose our side was more advanced than they let on. But I remember one day in particular. The man who sat up in the phone bank above the plotting board leaned over and called down, "Something's going to pass across in a minute far quicker than anything you've ever plotted before." And it did. It moved across the board very quickly - it was a type of jet engine that we were testing. RAF Cardington wasn't far away and that's where experimental aircraft were.'

As an early warning service, the ROC worked closely with Radar posts.

'We all had to know a great deal and we'd have tests. They'd hold up silhouettes head on and then lateral views and we'd have to write down what they were. We had to know. But the elderly men knew so much. They really were incredible.'

One of the benefits of being close to Bedford was the proximity of so many airmen, especially Americans. Not only did the RAF Dance Band play regularly at nearby RAF Cardington, but Glenn Miller was also based near the town.

'He was wonderful. He'd come and play at the Corn Exchange in Bedford and we'd go along there to dances just to hear him. We had a wonderful time in many ways. It was a terrible war but I wouldn't have missed it.'

In company with the majority, Shirley remembers the V1 as the most frightening weapon unleashed on Britain.

'You'd hear 'pop, pop, pop,' and then it'd cut out and then there would be an explosion. You never knew where they were going to land. They were very frightening. We could plot them but when the V2s started, they just came. We had no way at all of predicting them.'

After D-Day, the Royal Observer Corps was disbanded and Shirley was given a choice. Either join the WRNS, or return to civilian life and become a volunteer.

'The WRNS jobs was cooking - and I didn't want to do that. So I joined the Red Cross and went into the VAD's (Voluntary Aid Detachment). I worked at a local hospital and eventually, after it had all finished, became a radiographer at the Middlesex Hospital'.

Aunt Marie was partly French. She had maintained her contacts in Europe who kept her informed of life under German occupation. The four Jewish women she employed at her shop were a constant reminder of what was happening in Europe. But it was not until a visit to the cinema, at the very end of the war, that the full horror hit Shirley.

'I had an American boyfriend at the time and we'd gone to the pictures. A newsreel came on of the very first pictures of Belsen. I cannot describe how I felt, even to this day. Nobody said a word; you could have heard a pin drop in that cinema. Even when we were leaving, there was no sound other than people crying. I can remember that day like it was yesterday. Everybody was so shattered.'

The six years of war had brought about the start of tremendous social change. The barriers that had previously separated people and confined them within prescribed occupations, began to crumble. A chance remark overheard in the street made Shirley realise just how extraordinary those years had been.

'There was a chap who'd been a Mosquito pilot and

somebody said that before the war he'd been a Lloyds bank manager. And it suddenly struck me that we were all ordinary people fighting a war. In Civvie Street, this man had been a bank manager, but there he was flying planes and fighting. We were all just ordinary people'.

Shirley followed a career in medicine, had five children, and now lives in southern England.

CHAPTER TWENTY FOUR

Betty Kerr - Ambulance Driver

When she was seventeen, Betty Kerr had managed to save enough money to buy a second-hand car. A Standard Nine. Her aim was to join the London Ambulance Service.

'I loved driving and the Ambulance Service had lots of vehicles - and heavy ones at that. It was a great way to practise and so I went to the ambulance station in Belsize Park to do more of what I'd just learned and drive their ambulances.'

Betty had been with the Service for several months before war was declared and, by September, her skills were in great demand. Now at the forefront of the war effort, she was sent to the front line - a garage in Islington.

'There were three girls there and a very mixed bunch of men - taxi drivers, tradesmen and company directors. We covered 24 hours a day, driving cars and lorries that had been fitted with stretchers.'

All were volunteers and, like her, the two women she worked with were not local.

'Not many women drove in those days and certainly not in Islington. There was no animosity towards us at all.

There was a real spirit of pulling together and wanting to get on with things.'

After about eight months Betty decided to leave. She joined the First Aid Nursing Yeomanry - later known as the FANY's.

The FANY's offered interesting opportunities for work overseas and Betty knew girls who had been sent to India and Egypt. Excited by the prospect, she put her name down, increasing her age by two years to try and improve her chances.

'I wanted to drive - that was my main ambition - and most of the FANY's were drivers. But I also applied for them because the uniform was better!'

Accepted by them, she was despatched to Camberley to develop her driving skills. From there she was given her first posting.

'I was sent to Southend Hospital in Bristol. I stayed there for the next eighteen months, working in the Army blood supply company. It was all FANY's and we were all drivers.'

Betty's job was to drive a blood collecting team around the south west of England, collecting blood donations. Each team comprised a doctor, four nurses and an orderly. The doctor and nurses went in a car, the equipment followed in a lorry, driven by the not quite nineteen year-old Betty.

'We always had an assortment of lorries, depending on what was available. One we got quite fond of was a huge removal van and you had to stand out on the step to reverse it so you could see where you were going.'

As well as driving the vehicles, the women of the

Yeomanry also serviced them.

'In those days, most of the lorries had oil nipples underneath. We had to bleed those, as well as doing general servicing. We also had to crank vehicles with a handle to start them. That was very hard work but we just did it.'

Blood supplies were in high demand not only for those fighting overseas, but for the casualties at home. Collecting teams would visit villages and towns and 'bleed' them, usually in the village hall. The donation process became a symbol of public duty.

On one occasion, Betty witnessed, first hand, the spirit of the British people and their determination to survive, no matter what. The memory of that day will stay with her forever.

'I will never forget a 'bleed' in Plymouth - the day after it had been badly bombed. We were amazed at how many donors turned up. Many of them had bandaged limbs or heads from their own injuries from the night before.'

The bombardment of Britain had become so fierce and so frequent, that an invasion was not only expected, but believed to be imminent. Blood was a valuable and vital commodity, crucial to the survival of the country and something to be kept from an invading enemy at all costs.

'The blood that we collected in Plymouth that night had to be taken to Bristol and we took turns doing that. We were given an orderly with a rifle, in case the invasion started and the Germans tried to take our blood. We really thought that they would come at any time.'

But Germany turned its attention towards Russia. With the threat of an invasion waning, the FANY's amalgamated with the ATS.

Betty continued to drive an assortment of vehicles before accepting the challenge of promotion, from lance corporal, to corporal to sergeant. This not only gave her three stripes, it also earned her a motorbike.

'The ATS drivers were attached to an RASC company in Bournemouth and provided vehicles for young officers to practice their map reading skills. When the whole company moved, I was a courier for the convoy, riding my motorbike and checking that everyone kept up. I also manned the crossroads where necessary.'

Fortunately, there were no incidents and no stragglers on that convoy, and it reached its destination - Southend-on-Sea - without mishap.

Eventually, Betty earned a commission and was posted to Newcastle. Here she managed a platoon and kept tabs on an array of vehicles scattered all over Northumberland. One of her responsibilities was to inspect the field vehicles and ensure they were serviceable.

This new job gave her a lot of freedom but it also had its drawbacks. It was very uncomfortable work especially in the middle of the northern winter.

'I shall never forget how cold it was. I was out on the moors by myself and it was desolate. I wore gloves of course, but I still had to stop and try to thaw my hands on the exhaust pipe so that I could continue. I made these trips about once a month.'

In between, she supervised vehicle maintenance in Newcastle until, in 1942, now a subaltern, she asked to be posted south.

'The Blitz was in full swing and my parents were in

London. I felt really out of it up there, so I asked for a transfer and got South Kensington. I had a garage in the King's Road in Chelsea, and a platoon of assorted vehicles. We even had Queen Mary's old Daimler, as well as other staff cars that had been commandeered.'

In London she supervised transport for the War Office. Her unit drove senior civil servants and war office personnel.

As well as running the garage, it was Betty's responsibility to manage a block of flats off Sloane Square where many of the ATS drivers were billeted.

One of the decisions that tormented her most, was the welfare of her staff. As the officer in charge, she had to decide whether to wake them when a raid was imminent, or gamble that the enemy aircraft would be downed by ack-ack fire or the RAF.

'It was an awful responsibility on a night duty when we had air-raids to decide whether to get the girls up. We had use of the cellars but the girls needed their sleep in order to be on duty the next day.'

After a year in London, Betty finally got her overseas posting. She was despatched to Frankfurt, to General Eisenhower's HQ. After three weeks there, the whole contingent was sent to Versailles.

'I had a beautiful flat there, right next to the palace. It had high ceilings and was so beautifully decorated. I'd finally got the overseas work that I'd wanted all along but in just three months the war was over. And that was that!'

Betty now lives in Surrey.

CHAPTER TWENTY FIVE
Joy Schooley - Aircraft Engineer

Joy and Archibald Schooley from London got married in February 1939. After just a few months, Archibald joined the Army. Initially he had a home posting and Joy saw him fairly regularly. Then he was sent to North Africa.

When he enlisted, Joy realised that it was only a matter of time before she would be called to do war work. As a lone woman with no dependants, she could be sent anywhere. She decided to strike first.

'The Blitz was on and my flat had been bombed, and I'd seen this course advertised. My maths was quite good, so that's what I did.'

After a move to Lancashire and enrolment on a three-month engineering course, Joy got a job as an aircraft engineer with the Bristol Aircraft Company, then under the Ministry of Aircraft Production.

'We made just one engine - the Hercules; this went into Wellingtons, Stirlings, Halifaxes and the Beaufighter. I worked on the supercharger bit of it.'

Her exam results earned her promotion to inspector, with responsibility for checking work.

'My job was to make sure things were right. Everything had to be perfect and, if it wasn't, it was out. If you got it wrong, the engine would fail. This was no good either for the war effort or the poor pilot. We inspectors had to be sure and that's why we were separated - so as you couldn't pass your own work if it wasn't good enough. It was very interesting but, if I'm honest, I would have loved to have actually made some of the bits. As it was, I only had to sign it off.'

Engine production was a specialist skill, requiring patience, attention to detail, and consistency.

'Everything was ground and the surfaces had to be perfect. Perfectly round, perfectly smooth. They had to fit together exactly and it was all etched.'

The ongoing fighting meant that Joy's department was constantly under pressure to increase production. However, the process was frequently held up by factors beyond their control.

'At the time I joined, we were often waiting for parts that we needed to make the rest of the engine. All the stuff we made fitted together in this big case thing called a volute.'

Despite escalating demand, quality still had to be assured. Substandard work was likely to cost lives, but some of the men proved to be too heavy-handed for precision engineering.

'These men had been "tacklers" in the mill days. They'd been the men who'd fixed the machines for the women, and that often needed brute force. The mill women worshipped them because if the machines stopped, they lost money, so they made up to them. Tacklers thought they were gods and they didn't like it when I turned their work down. They'd do things like bash these beautifully ground surfaces with ordinary hammers instead of tapping them with the lightweight hide ones. And that was no good.'

While the job was not difficult, the conditions in which they lived and worked were.

'The weather was a real shock to me. We were in this old spinning mill near Clitheroe and it was so cold. I'd never seen snow like it and, for the last eighteen months, I worked permanent nights just so I could get up in the warm, work in the warm and go to bed in the warm. It was bitter.'

And then there was the factory.

'The gaps under the floorboards were filled with textile fibres - they used to call it "dawn." I didn't know what it was at first but then I realised it was spinning leftovers. Well, the floors were oily and everything was cleaned in this fine paraffin spray. It's a wonder we didn't all go up in smoke.'

Being from the South, Joy was an outsider. Whilst there was a willingness to pull together, the local women's behaviour and dress code was not what she was used to.

'I'd always dressed properly and kept my hair nice, wore a bit of make-up. That's just how it was where I came from. But some of these women, they came to work in curlers and all sorts. I'd never seen anything like it. And I spoke differently, too, coming from London. They used to call me "Lady Schooley." They thought I was posh just because I brushed my teeth!'

But the women were hard-working and the barriers eventually fell.

'We worked twelve hour shifts but we did have a laugh.

We had this stuff called engineers' blue - it was some sort of inky lubricant. You'd often see people walking around with blue circles round their eyes where they'd looked through an eyepiece that somebody had inked.'

It was then discovered that one of the pieces of equipment had another use.

'On nights it was a bit more relaxed although we still worked just as hard. Somebody discovered that the little paint drying ovens were quite good for cooking and that meant they could have hot food for dinner, so they started putting pies in there. Then one night a boss came in, looked in the oven and found one cooking. There was an awful to do over that!'

Aircraft production was essential work and this meant the factory had its own Home Guard, another source of amusement for Joy and her companions.

'They really were like Dad's Army. They were all elderly men and they used to go out on their manoeuvres at dinner time - during the night. We used to tease them but they were always so serious. I remember them all lined up in the dark one night and the one in charge shouted: "Right you men, remember the ren-dez-vos is zero one hundred hours". It was so funny.'

Despite the laughs, hardship was routine. Having been bombed out of her flat before she moved to Lancashire, Joy had put her salvaged possessions into storage, only to lose them in a robbery.

'I had to go down to London and see what was what. It was right in amongst all the bombing that was going on but I had to see what was left and was gone.'

However, losing possessions seemed a minor

inconvenience when compared to those who lost everything.

'My sister in law and I both boarded with a woman who had two small children. The woman's husband was with bomb disposal and he'd just got a stripe. She wasn't much good at sewing so, the week before, I'd sewn his stripe on for her. When a telegram came, I said without thinking: "Your husband's coming home." But he wasn't. It was to say he'd been killed. It was heartbreaking - atrocious.'

From casual lodger, Joy had become a friend.

'What made it worse was that his mum lived nearby. I had to take the two small children round to her and tell her that her son had been killed. Awful.'

Joy began to feel dogged by death. Guilt set in.

'I felt like I was taking doom with me. After this woman's husband had been killed, we had to move and we went to a little stone one-up, one-down place with this other young woman. Her husband was a pilot and he was killed while we were with her. You didn't know what to say to people. They're here today and gone tomorrow. I think I was the first one to have a loss, after that it was all deaths.'

In December 1943, Joy's husband had been captured, although word did not reach her until January 1944.

'I last saw him on Halloween 1943 in Scotland, but that was it for two and a half years. It was a worry. I never used to worry after myself but I did worry about him, if he was all right.'

Albert Schooley remained a prisoner until a month after the war in Europe had finished.

'The Russians finally let his camp out. I remember him

telling me about the release. He said they could see something coming but they didn't know what it was. It turned out to be Cossacks on horseback, bobbing up and down in the mist.'

But her husband's experience as a prisoner had changed him irrevocably.

'He'd lost an awful lot of weight and I think what hurt me most was how, after a meal, he'd scoop up all the crumbs from the tablecloth and eat them. He'd changed, and it never left him.'

Joy Schooley now lives in East Sussex.

CHAPTER TWENTY SIX

Anne McHugh - Airframe Carpenter

A native of Lancashire, in her mid-teens Anne McHugh had moved south to Berkshire. In the 1930s, Reading was a largely rural environment, with only isolated areas of light industry.

'I worked at Huntley and Palmers - the biscuit people. That was just near to where we lived. I did clerical work there, learning it as I went along, then I got married in 1939 and, in those days, you didn't work. You stayed at home and, looked after your husband. Well, that's what you were supposed to do.'

Husband or not, Anne was eventually called up for war work and sent to nearby Woodley Aerodrome. This was the home of the Miles Aircraft Company and a base for training aircraft. She was sent to the wood shop to be a carpenter.

'I'd never handled a tool or done anything like that before, but we were seen by inspectors and given things to make. Depending on how you got on, you were given jobs. I made a toolbox with sliding drawers. I went to "Repair and Service" with five other girls but I was the one who stayed the longest. I liked the work - loved it.'

Whilst she may have enjoyed it and was both ready and willing to learn all she could about being a carpenter, Anne could not have been prepared for the conditions to which she was subjected, or the behaviour of her male colleagues.

'They were all ages, the men, and I was alone amongst men who hated women workers. It was nothing to do with me personally but I took it as very personal. They were very against girls in the aircraft industry.'

The airframe industry was a reserved occupation. Some of the men were also medically unfit or too old for active service. As well as carpentry, their job was the induction and training of the women, but male pride frequently prevented them from treating their trainees as equals.

'They'd do things like if you were even one minute late, they would stand there knocking the benches in time with their hammers. And they'd stare at you. Watch your every move so that you always felt very silly.'

It was an atmosphere of intimidation that increased as the day progressed.

'I was allotted to one man who had to show me what to do, train me. But he never spoke to me. No "Good morning, good afternoon" or anything. Nothing. None of them. He'd go off to chat to the men or go for stores, but he never spoke to me except to tell me I'd done something wrong, or to tell me to do something. He was always very rude to me'

Anne and the other women were shunned. Nobody spoke to them and they were left out of every part of factory life except the actual work. Ostracised, the atmosphere gradually intensified until, one-by-one, the women left.

Only Anne McHugh remained. And she had no intention of giving in. On her own, she bore the brunt of their silent contempt.

'Everything was always aimed at me, but I stuck it because I liked the work. My favourite job was patching the aircraft body. You had to patch it so that it all matched. It was like a jigsaw really. I had all my own tools and I loved it. But it was a very lonely life, especially after all the other girls had gone.'

One day, after enduring six months amongst her hostile colleagues, something happened that she could not have foreseen.

'I came into work and it was all quiet. The men were all there - they must have come in extra early because I wasn't late. I had a drawer for my tools and things, and I opened it to put my handbag in. As I did, there was a snake, all curled up. They'd put it in there obviously expecting me to yell but I didn't. No hysterics or anything; I just shut the drawer very quietly, didn't say anything, and went off to do the plane'

The men had found the grass snake in a nearby field. But their prank fell flat; Anne merely got on with her work. The following day, the man with whom she worked, the same man who had never spoken to her other than to give her orders, came over to her.

'I was inside a plane, upside down under the top, fixing a patch. He came up and said, "Sweet?" He had a bag of sweets and he was pushing them towards me, clearly embarrassed and not wanting anybody else to see. I looked in astonishment, amazed he'd spoken to me and that here was a sweet for me - a woman! I took one. It was the first time he'd ever spoken to me other than with an order. Then he said, "I'm sorry about that" and I knew he meant the snake. You could have knocked me down with a feather!'

After that, the atmosphere lightened. It was clear that her tormentors had finally given up trying to break her. Eventually, she was included in their lunchtime visits to the local pub.

'I was very lonely before. They'd go to the pub and I was left on my own. Sometimes I'd go for a little walk on the airfield, or sometimes I'd just eat my lunch by myself, then go back to work when they returned. There were no other girls there. I was never included. But after the snake, I felt that I became quite popular and had proved myself by standing up to them.'

Accepted she might have been, but she still only received a fraction of the wage paid to the men for doing the same job.

'You just accepted what you were given as a woman. It wasn't a woman's world then. Nothing like today. I thought about giving up many times, but I liked the work, and I had to do something, and anyway, I wasn't going to be beaten by those silly men.'

Like many of her contemporaries, Anne enjoyed the social opportunities the war years offered, workshop conditions notwithstanding. They held dances and organised house parties to entertain themselves, and made the best of their lives. But the war was never far away.

When she left the aerodrome she went to work at the Green Monkey pub with a friend. It was a regular haunt of many young men who had been badly burned and who were being treated by the pioneering plastic surgeon, Sir Archibald McIndoe.

'Some were a really dreadful sight but we didn't care. Just because they were in a bad state why shouldn't we help them? They'd stop in on their way to the races and have a meal - a lunch or a dinner - and sometimes we'd have dances there with them. You know, just be there for them.'

At the end of the war, life gradually regained some of its normality. But many of the old prejudices that had shaped attitudes towards women remained. Anne decided it was time to move on. She settled back into married life and raised two children. And the tool kit? She gave it away.

Anne still lives near Reading.

CHAPTER TWENTY SEVEN

Vera Wilson - Factory Worker

'Mum was in the kitchen and I remember her shouting, "War's started, war's started!"
Vera Wilson had just turned fourteen. As an only child, she lived in Belvedere, south east London, with her parents. Her father worked on the Thames Estuary in a reserved occupation, at the Crossness sewerage outfall.
As a young girl just embarking on working life, she remembers those early months of 1939 as a strange time.
'Not long after it all began, the sirens went and we all rushed down the shelters but it was a false alarm. There was a plane but they didn't know if it German or not. But things just carried on as normal really.'
War or no war, life in the workplace did not start well.
'I started at Grooms. That was at Belvedere. We used to make fish paste and fill mustard tins but I got the sack from there. We were playing in the yard, a group of us, and I threw a ball to one of the boys but he missed it and the foreman came round the corner. It caught him smack in the face. So that was me sacked. Me and another girl. '
Fortunately, this indiscretion had not made Vera totally unemployable.

'We went to the Co-op after that, picking strawberries and topping and tailing gooseberries ready for jams and that. My father always wanted me to go to Burroughs and Wellcome at Dartford but they didn't take you until you were sixteen.'

With men called up for active service and women being required to do war work, vacancies arose in places that would have remained out of reach for many.

'My friend got a job at Burroughs - and she was only fifteen. So she came and told us about it and that's how I got in there early. I was in Dad's good books too.'

Burroughs and Wellcome made pills and powdered medicines. All workers wore white coats, hair nets and gloves. They were also required to take a dark coat to the floor where they worked.

'I was on the fourth floor and, when the sirens went off, we had to run down the stairs, round the yard and down to the shelters. Well, being all in white, we were easy targets especially when we had to dash across the open yard. So the dark coat was to make us less visible to the Germans because they did shoot at people on the ground. And they'd be able to see where the shelters were.'

Despite the ever present danger, Vera and many others developed a somewhat blasé attitude towards raids.

'The sirens went off one day and we got outside but then we noticed there was a big dogfight going on right above. So we stood there cheering and waving our fists at the Germans. But the foreman came after us and started chasing us down into the shelters. I don't think we really thought anything would ever happen to us.'

But a few weeks later, one busy Saturday morning in

nearby Bexleyheath, something happened that changed her mind.

'A German plane flew down the Broadway and strafed people shopping. I remember hearing about it and realising that it could happen. There were lots of people killed - women and children, all machine gunned by this bloody German plane.'

Later in the war, when Vera and her mother were returning from seeing her aunt and three children off at the railway station, the Germans visited Belvedere.

'The station got hit and we were just up the street. We flattened ourselves against the wall and should really have gone down a shelter, but we kept running for home. There was fighting overhead and bombs dropping all round, but we thought we'd be better off dying at home. It was silly really, we could have got hit or blasted or cut up by flying glass and shrapnel, but we kept running. Daft really.'

As the war progressed and Vera reached eighteen, she decided to enlist. However, her efforts were thwarted by her parents, notably her mother.

'Mum said, "You're not going. If you're going to die, you'll die here with us." And that was that. I was an only child, and by this time I suppose we'd all seen what the Germans got up to and I suppose Mum was worried what would happen to me. She used to shake during the air raids, she was scared stiff. So I suppose that was fair enough.'

Instead, Vera diverted her energies towards work more directly linked to the war effort. Vickers aircraft factory was at nearby Crayford and her uncle, who already worked there on a job of National importance, secured her a place.

'I started there on my eighteenth birthday, making armatures for the Navy. These were parts that went into the casing of compasses, and we used to wind them. But when we ran out, I was sent to do aircraft dials.'

Her job entailed laboriously painting the numbers and markers on dials for flight controls, instruments and fuel gauges. Each one was moulded and Vera had to fill in each number clearly with white paint. It was very slow work, done with a fine brush and, eager to help the war effort, she was delighted when somebody suggested a method of speeding up such a tiresome chore. 'Somebody said to put white paint right over it, let it dry and then clean it off. But, of course, what I didn't realise was that when I cleaned it, all the black paint would come off too. I mucked 'em all up and I got told off over that. But I was forgiven. I didn't do it again, mind!'

Despite that incident, she resisted any further attempts to streamline her working processes, but she did succumb to another suggestion.

'I started smoking. Every time I went to a bench they'd offer me a cigarette. I refused at first, but then I tried and I was hooked. Everybody smoked then, and after that I carried on for years. I only gave up about fifteen years ago. Naughty, very naughty.'

Belvedere lies between Kent and the south eastern perimeter of London, directly on the line of approach for any planes making for the capital. Vickers main factory was at Crayford but the demand for aircraft components prompted the acquisition of additional premises. It also meant that if hit, production would not cease completely. One such place was set up close to where Vera lived.

'We got bombed at the works - it rattled our place and all the glass came out. We dived under the benches. That time it was a landmine and it exploded one dinnertime.'

Unfortunately for the inhabitants of her street, the explosion occurred just as many of them were returning to the factory.

'Two or three people who lived up our road were killed. We had friends - Mr and Mrs Torry who lived a couple of doors up. Mr Torry was killed as well as another man. The Torrys were really nice people. And that same time there were quite a few from nearby roads - not friends as such but neighbours and acquaintances.'

Then, on a visit to the cinema, Vera herself narrowly escaped injury.

'The pub opposite got a direct hit. I remember they made everybody from the circle come down into the stalls as it was unsafe but the film just carried on. You couldn't let it stop you doing things or else you'd never have done anything. Then when the film finished, there were fire engines outside and all the flames were going right up. I just got on my bus and went home. That's what you did.'

For many who lived through it, life in the air-raid shelters was a trial.

'We were down there every night and our next door but one neighbours used to come in, too. Dad often worked shifts so it was me, Mum, the dog and the neighbours. They were from up north and she had a lovely singing voice. We used to sing all night, especially when it got very noisy and the guns were all going. Poor old Mum was always scared - of the Germans, not the singing. I wasn't frightened - I don't think that when you're young you really realise what it's all about. We never got much sleep though.'

And Vera's dog was the best early warning system that the Wilsons' could have had.

'The dog was always down there first; he could hear the planes, even before the sirens went off. He'd howl at the door wanting to go out and if you opened it, he'd be straight down the shelter, and Mum'd shout," The Germans are coming, the Germans are coming!" and we'd go after him. Then the sirens would go off. It was funny really.'

But not night after night and especially not when they returned during the day. This continued for over six months and, by the end of it, many people were close to exhaustion.

Meanwhile, life went on. Vera recalled trading rations with women at work who had children to feed.

'Lots of people kept rabbits and chickens, but didn't want butter and stuff. We used to give out rabbits at Christmas. Sometimes I'd buy butter at work off people who didn't want it, and take it home for Mum.'

Occasionally, a little mistake meant a rare treat.

'I remember once the woman in Woolies accidentally gave me double the ration of tea. Normally I would have told her, but I knew how much Mum liked this particular tea, so I kept quiet and ran out of the shop in case the woman came after me. She didn't, though.'

For Vera, the war that had started when she was a child, finished when she was a young woman. Like many of her contemporaries, she lived through danger, rationing, shortages and constant disruption. Yet it all ended as suddenly as it had started.

'After the war, Vickers moved back to Crayford and shut the little place up the road. That meant I had to travel there every day, but it didn't matter. Things were still all over the place but at least we got a good night's sleep once it finished.'

Vera now lives near Maidstone in Kent.

CHAPTER TWENTY EIGHT

Olive Walker - Factory Worker

Olive Walker was born in Clacton in the East End of London. When she was four, the family moved to Leyton, where they spent the entire war - mother, father, Olive and her sister.

In January 1940, at fourteen, she started work in a box factory in Leytonstone. But instead of the chocolate boxes she had been expecting, she found herself making less ornate items.

'When I first started there, they were making fancy things. But then there was so much packaging wanted for the Forces - for the vials and the medicines and all that - we started doing padded boxes. We knew they were for the Forces. We bent them into shape and covered them, separated them into little sections and made sure they'd be OK.'

In those early years of the war, many women just absorbed the changes that were made to their normal jobs. It was only after the war had finished that many of them realised the significance of their efforts.

'We were just making boxes like we usually did. I never thought I'd done much but as the years went on, and you hear things, you realise that we all did our bit. OK, we didn't fight, but we still got bombed and shot at and buggered about. That was just how it all was then.'

Had it not been for those at home seemingly 'doing nothing', the men fighting would not have had the medical supplies, the ammunition or the aeroplanes they so badly needed.

In the beginning, life just carried on and nothing much seemed to happen. Then the Blitz began. Olive, like many other Londoners, was hurled into a daily ritual of danger, uncertainty and destruction, all mixed in with the ordinariness of everyday life.

'When the Blitz started, none of us was prepared for what was going to happen. The sirens would go off at about nine at night and Dad would go out into the garden to look for the searchlights. You could see them criss-crossing about and you knew that meant they were on the way. The radio always dimmed about that time and it was a signal. We'd get our bits and pieces together and go down the shelter. Ours was down the garden.'

At first, the raids were only at night but then they came during the day. The disruption meant, for many, a thinner pay packet at the end of the week.

'It was all piece work, so if we had a daytime raid, we had to stop work, go down the shelters and stay there 'til it was all over. And if you didn't work, you didn't get paid and that was that. It was bad enough having all your stuff blown up and blasted time and time again but not being able to replace 'cos you had no money - that was really hard.'

After the interruptions of the day, they went home to prepare for the night.

'We'd come in, have our tea, have a wash and that, get our bits together. If we were lucky, we'd go out, but it all had to be ready because we knew they'd come, and you had to be quick when they did.'

During those months, Olive spent fifty-seven consecutive nights in the shelter. It was cold and damp, and condensation ran down the metal walls.

'They came in waves. It was all quiet at first and we'd sit there thinking perhaps they wouldn't come that maybe the coastal guns had shot them down or they'd turned back. But they always did. That waiting was the worst bit. You'd hear this heavy droning in the distance and it'd get louder and, sometimes, it was as if the whole German Air Force was up there. Then the guns and the bombs would start and the noise. The whole of Leyton seemed to be shaking and banging. I can remember trembling and thinking: "Will I survive this?" I did - we all, did but not everybody was as lucky.'

Part of the terror was finding out who had been caught up in the night's destruction.

'In the morning, there was this awful smell of brick dust and burning. I walked past the devastation on the way to work and I always dreaded getting there and finding out who was missing. There was always some poor bugger. People didn't turn up and then you'd find out. We were always collecting for wreaths.'

Destruction seemed to surround them.

'I remember coming out of the front door one morning after a bad raid and seeing five coffins going by - one after the other. You'd often see one or two, but seeing all five in a line - it was a whole family, wiped out, just like that.'

But there was humour, too.

'We had an outside toilet and during the night you'd have to go. We'd try and nip out between waves but poor old Mum seemed to cop it every time. Just as she got in there, they'd come back and we'd be shouting at her to come back quick. You couldn't even do that in peace!'

Frequently, the effects of blast were as bad as the actual bombs. Most air-raid shelters had earth piled on top of them to afford not only extra protection, but camouflage. Many people also grew food on them - the warmth from the occupants giving a boost to the vegetables that supplemented the meagre war-time rations. People learned to be resourceful and Olive's mother recognised the potential to feed her family.

'She had this marrow and it was growing well. One night a bomb dropped two streets away. Come the morning, the blast had blown all the earth off, and the marrow was gone. Poor old Mum was right upset. We spent about an hour looking for it but we couldn't find it. A couple of hours later, when she opened the front door to pay the milkman, there was the marrow on the front doorstep. It had been blown right over the house. Mind you, it was a bit bashed up and we couldn't eat it.'

Many people also grew food on allotments.

'Ours was right on Hackney Marshes, next to the river which was handy for watering. In the summer we'd go down there and spend the evenings sitting around the shed while Dad weeded. But when the V1's started, one landed on the riverbank and blew the shed up.'

Everyone lived with tiredness and discomfort yet,

despite the nightly disturbance, people still got up for work.

'It was too noisy to sleep and I was too scared to in case I didn't wake up. But you just dozed as best you could. We were always shattered but there was no let up. You had to get on with it and hope you would get a bit more rest the next night. It was just one of those things but we'd laugh and gee each other up at work to get through.'

And then there was the Brussels Sprouts incident.

'We knew the marshes had got it, and when we got down there, there was all these stalks still in the ground - but no sprouts. The blast had blown them clean off. We never did find any!'

Aside from the daily interruptions and difficulties that had to be endured, life carried on, almost as normal. When Olive's Aunt Lil got married, there was a church service, a reception and an iced wedding cake. Unfortunately, the noise of an air-raid made the service hard to hear. Then there was the bomb that blew up the reception party, covering the cake in plaster, the guests in soot and smashing the bottles that had been collected to toast the happy couple.

Olive's own engagement was also affected by the war.

'Arthur was in North Africa and he sent me money for my ring. When I bought it I wrote and we arranged to get engaged at a certain time. He was in the Royal Signals and he could get the BBC - he wasn't supposed to, mind. Anyway, come the day, we both tuned into Big Ben at nine o'clock, but just before I suddenly said: "I can't put me own ring on." So I asked Dad to do it for me and that's how we got engaged. Me and Arthur got married in 1946 and we're still together now.'

Talk to anyone from those long years of war and they claim they got used to it. But mention the doodlebugs and the reaction is common to all.

'We sort of got used to bombs and the noise, but those flying bombs were horrible. You never knew what was going to happen. That shook it all up again. You tried to live normally but there was all these interruptions that you had no control over.'

The silent immediacy of the V2 rockets, launched from mainland Europe, introduced yet another chilling facet to the fighting.

'We were all working one day in the factory when there was this bright orange flash that lit up the whole department. It was one of those rockets. There was no warning. Anyway, the ARP phoned and said it had hit the Leyton High Road - well, that was me.'

Told to go home, Olive remembers how she felt as she put her coat on.

'I was all jittery and as I got nearer home the devastation got worse - there were fires and curtains out the windows, children crying, ambulances and all that. I was dreading what I was going to find.'

As she reached her house, her worst fears were confirmed. The house was still standing but it had been badly damaged. There was no sign of her mother.

'I walked up the alley and into the back garden. There was nobody about and I thought: "God, where's Mum?"

'The window frames were hanging in. The ceilings were down, the clock was halfway up the passage. Mum had been cooking and there was a basin of dripping on the side that had burst and was all running down. The front door was laying down, I just didn't know what to do, really. I couldn't see Mum anywhere.'

Fortunately, her mother had escaped serious injury and had left the house to make sure her other daughter, working nearby in a shop, was unhurt.

'Mum had gone and fetched Dad. She'd cleared up so much debris from the blast before that she felt that she just couldn't cope with it again. We just didn't know where to start. I mean, she'd salvaged all Gran's stuff when she'd been bombed out, then there was that fiasco at Aunt Lil's wedding. I think this time, it was just too much for her.'

The house was patched-up by friends and neighbours so the family could move back in. It was finally demolished by developers in the 1960's.

Olive now lives in Surrey.

CHAPTER TWENTY NINE

Doreen Lloyd - Bank Worker

Doreen Lloyd's birth during a Zeppelin raid in 1917 was the only major event in her early years; the rest passed remarkably smoothly until the late 1930s.

In 1935, she started work in the stationery department of Lloyds Bank, then situated in Park Royal, London NW10. By 1938 it was clear that the tension in Europe was growing. The National Socialist Party had a firm hold on Germany and in Britain many were uneasy. When war was finally declared on September 3rd 1939, it came as no real surprise to Doreen Lloyd.

The early days were spent in preparation. The sewing of blackout curtains, taping of windows to reduce blast damage and the sandbagging of public buildings provided a focus for what was to come. But for Doreen, it was not until the following summer, with the fall of France, that she and a friend decided to enlist.

'We wanted to be plotters - there was a plotting station in Northwood, which wasn't far away. But anything would do that would help the war effort.'

On August 5th 1940, they both went to AD Astral House in Kingsway, the RAF recruiting point.

'We had our applications to join the WAAF all filled in and ready, and after a preliminary interview we were sent behind the screens for our medical. She was accepted; I was turned down.'

This incident was one of the worst days of her life. The two women had been friends since school and they had hoped to stay together. Unfortunately, Doreen had failed the eyesight test, and her application was stamped 'unfit'.

'I wore glasses and couldn't read the first words on the test card without them. I remember I was gutted; I felt terrible - how could they have turned me down, especially after I'd been kind enough to offer my services to a needy government!'

As far as Doreen's military career was concerned, that seemed to be that. She returned to her job in the bank and waited to see what developed.

'The first daylight raids on the docklands area of London began and, as September wore on, so the raids became more intense. The weekend of the twenty-ninth and thirtieth was a very active one. Despite the war, it had been business as usual, with people working around inconvenience. Customers still had money and investments to be managed, regardless of world politics. But on Monday I arrived at Ealing Broadway station to find there were no trains. A stick of bombs had dropped, taking out the District, Central London and GWR Railways. And the Uxbridge trolley buses could get no further than Ealing Common.'

There was no option but to walk to North Acton. It took Doreen almost an hour, but when she got to the office, she was only the third person to arrive - out of a staff of seventy.

Where her office building had stood on Friday night, there were now just four walls and smouldering debris. The area had received the full force of the bombing.

'When the manager finally arrived, he tried to find a phone that was working. He eventually found one in a café and reported the position to Head Office in Lombard Street. We were told to return home and, as and when the railways were working again, report to H.O.'

Those who had struggled to work through the devastated streets now had to walk home again, back through the chaos, braving the danger of falling masonry and unexploded bombs.

It is easy to overlook the efforts of those engaged in work of National importance, but it was the combined industry of everybody, from all walks of life, that helped the country survive, and made the tasks of those nearer the front line a little easier.

Jobs of National importance were part of the foundation upon which the country depended. And that dependence often emerged from initiative, determination and invention born out of necessity.

Between October and December that year, Doreen resumed her work at the bank's Head Office in Central London, helping to rectify the damage.

'We had to reconstruct everything. We had no files or records left as everything had been burnt in the fires caused by the bombing. We were given some trestle tables and we set about contacting all the branch banks and getting them to send us duplicate files '

However, as the year dragged on and the nights drew in,

the task became harder and harder as they had less and less daylight in which to operate. It was at night that the heaviest bombing usually took place.

'We had to leave early so that we could get home, have our supper and do what we could in our homes before the raids started. We had our main meals in the canteen at lunchtime. And anyway, from three o'clock the platforms on the Central Line stations from Bank to Shepherds Bush filled up with people seeking shelter.'

With the country firmly at war, the need to save resources and recycle anything that could be reused became increasingly important. One wartime measure was to save paper. The bank was no different, and staff began to recycle envelopes for inter-branch letters.

'We used to slit them open, flatten them out and then type on the back. It meant that we could save the bank's paper for customer correspondence. We also reused envelopes by fixing gummed labels to them for as long as they lasted.'

By the end of 1940, Doreen decided to leave the City.

'Our Ealing home had been damaged by a landmine exploding in the garden of the house opposite, our windows had been patched up and slates that had been dislodged from the roof were letting in water when it rained. And we had to spend every night in the cellar. So in early November, we moved to my grandmother's house at Ewell in Surrey.'

The move meant she had to travel overground by train to Waterloo, and return again in the evenings in a blacked out carriage lit only by blue lights.

In February 1941, Doreen began work for an Australian

Bank in Oxshott, a few miles from her grandmother's house. Several Australian banks and mining companies had taken over Sandroyd School (now Reed's School). Still involved with individual and corporate finance, Doreen also found time to do voluntary work.

'This was mostly in first-aid posts or in local canteens, but each Monday evening after work I went to the YMCA canteen at Waterloo Station. I used to catch the last train home; it left at 10.10 p.m. It took a week for my hands to recover from washing up the crockery in the soda that was put into the water - there were no rubber gloves then.'

The community in Ewell made their own entertainment, coped with the shortage of clothing and found ways to make food rations stretch.

'I mastered the art of making a pretty good sponge sandwich cake out of dried egg and carried on with life as normally as possible. We also did our fire-watching rota.'

Eventually, the air-raids became less frequent and it became easier for people to get around.

'If we went up to London in the evening for social reasons, such as seeing friends on leave, going to the theatre - they started at seven o'clock and finished by ten - or for any other activities and the sirens went off, we would wait until the ack-ack guns started up in the park or until we heard the noise of aircraft before going down to the underground stations until the all clear went. We were getting pretty blasé by then.'

Then, almost as if he had discovered their attitude, Hitler introduced the V1 and the V2 rockets.

'These started in about May 1944 and were a little

problematical as there was very little warning, especially at night. You only heard the drone of the V1 engine until it cut out. Then you dived under the nearest table. It's said that one never hears the bomb that hits you - well, no, of course not but I can confirm that you don't hear the near miss either.'

Doreen had her own near miss in the summer of 1944. During the week she stayed at Sandroyd, where dormitories had been built for staff. There was also a canteen in the grounds, equipped with a well-stocked bar, dartboard, snooker table and table tennis.

'On this particular evening, time had been called and I'd taken a lime juice up to bed. On realising I'd left my book in the office, I went to get it. And as I did, I heard the drone of a V1. Then it cut out and I dived under the office table. The next thing I knew, there was total silence. Every door was flat on the floor, the ceilings were on the tabletops and the windows were hanging from their frames.'

Apart from being covered in dust, she was unhurt and went outside to see what damage had been caused.

'The V1 had glided down towards the grounds but it had caught a few trees between the main building and the block for the canteen staff. It had exploded laterally. Fortunately, there were no casualties and the ARPs, police and fire fighters were soon with us.'

The following day, Doreen's office was evacuated. The other organisations returned to their London offices, but Lloyds leased a large house nearby. They stayed there until the end of the war, just over six months later.

Despite Doreen's lucky escape, others she knew had not

fared so well. Two years previously in 1942, her boyfriend had been killed on his way back from a raid over Bremen.

'1942 was the worse year (of the war) for me. So many people that I knew were killed. A friend's husband was killed in a daylight raid over Paris on May 29th and then my boyfriend was shot down. He had to ditch in the North Sea and was washed up in Holland. Now when I go to Runnymeade, to the memorial of the many with no known grave, I know so many of them.'

In spite of the tragedies of those six years, she still has fond memories of her life then.

'We became very adept at making do and I have un-picked and re-knitted many a sweater and cardigan; restyled numerous dresses and obtained materials through advertisements in 'The Lady' where no coupons were involved. We managed to grow runner beans in our garden which my grandmother, being a country-born girl, would patiently string and slice into a large bread crock, putting salt between each layer. This lasted us almost throughout the winter months.'

She also maintained a good social life, although it did have one major draw back.

'I started smoking mainly because when friends and relatives from the Forces came home on leave, they always brought cigarettes as gifts because they got them through the NAFFI and they were cheap. I finally kicked the habit in the 1950s.'

Smoking aside, Doreen views her war years as generally healthy.

'It was always a bonus for our rations when we went out to dinner to a restaurant where the standard charge for a two course meal was five shillings - old money - although they could charge up to one pound for a cup of coffee! For special occasions it was worth it. We were, in fact, very well-fed and finished the war healthier than we'd started it in many cases. There were few sweets and we used unbleached flour for the 'National Loaf' and butter and oil were very scarce.'

Doreen now lives in Surrey.

CIVIL DEFENCE

Britain's survival depended on everybody. Even after their regular day had finished, many people volunteered for additional work.

Civil Defence included air raid precautions (ARP) duties, firewatching, the Local Defence Volunteer Reserve (the Home Guard) and the WVS. Staffed by women and men too old to fight, unavailable or unfit for active duty, it also included those engaged in work of National importance, or reserved occupations.

With every incident requiring emergency action, there was rarely time to argue the suitability of gender. Nor did the debate of unequal pay feature; most civil defence work was unpaid. Volunteers acted as the eyes and ears of the community, supporting and assisting the National Fire Service and the police.

The threat of invasion and the search for downed enemy airmen presented a real purpose for would-be soldiers. Many LDF volunteers were old soldiers from the Great War. Others were ordinary citizens seeking to focus their feelings.

Surrounded by red tape and indecision, yet anxious to protect their homes and family, many women formed their own groups. Unbound by formal organisation, these women developed message networks, made weapons and learned how to sabotage, poison, booby trap and ambush. Some also learned to shoot. Fortunately, few needed to test their skills.

CHAPTER THIRTY

Joan Crump - Auxiliary Fire Service

Croydon in Surrey lies about fifteen miles south of London. Between the wars, it was the centre of world aviation, a centrepiece of British influence, the place from where Amy Johnson made many of her famous flights. Anybody who was anybody, flew from Croydon Airport.

On its own, it would have been a key target for the Luftwaffe but its position at the head of the Wealden Corridor and its proximity to Kenley, Biggin Hill and Redhill aerodromes, meant it was a primary objective.

In 1940, Joan Crump was living with her parents in East Drive, Shirley, a suburban village close to Croydon. As her mother was against her only child joining the Armed Forces, Joan opted instead for civil defence work.

'Mother had a friend who worked for the Auxiliary Fire Service and she got me an interview. I went for a test and got in.'

That was the start of Joan's war. A war that was to revolve around the mobilising of men and equipment in a deadly game of cat and mouse under daily fire.

'We really copped it in Croydon. We had the bombs first and then the doodlebugs. It was doodlebug alley and because of where we were, we had all these barrage balloons around Croydon. The flying bombs would get tangled up in them as they went for the City. They came down on us. One night, we had over two hundred fires in Croydon. The sky was that bright that you could see the pilots in the planes, all lit up.'

Each air-raid began a strategic sequence of manoeuvres in which Joan played a key part.

'We had to know as much as the men. It was our job to know what went on each appliance, what was needed and we had to make sure it was all there, ready to go. We worked in shifts and slept at the station. When the bell went off, we all just dived for the pole and slid into action. I became more or less permanent watch room.'

While the men went off to the fires, the women moved crews to places where they could provide the best cover, should they be needed.

'We always had to be ready for anything. You never knew where the next fire was going to be and once an engine was out, we moved others to cover. We had to plot it all, and tell them where to go. One night I remember particularly well. The West Wickham boys - West Wickham is just up the road from Shirley - were moved up towards London. The planes were going over, dropping their bombs, and these boys booked in to me. Off they went towards London and they got about a mile up the road, just past our crew, when they got blown up. All killed. I was the last one to see them alive. I'd only just spoken to them.'

The stations were old, with control rooms in the cellars, next to the furnace.

'It was so hot down there and in big raids we had to

wear gas masks. These went over the phone so you could talk into it. But it was so hot, you could hardly breathe.'

Being in the thick of the action, control room staff had to know the procedures back to front and stay close to the shelter.

'But it was no good to us. We had to stay where we were and deal with the fires. How could we have gone into the shelter - who would have done the work?'

It seems this important point had been overlooked when the instructions had been written.

In some ways, being a local girl was a great advantage because the streets were familiar. But it also meant that she knew many of the people affected by the bombing. These were real people, whose lives were being ripped apart night after night.

'Every time there was a raid, one of the men would go into the tower and spot where the bombs were landing. They usually got it within a couple of streets. One night they came down in Shirley - on my house - and I was in the control room. We could see the bombs falling on my house.'

The danger outside forced Joan to stay put, until she could stand it no longer.

'Eventually, I got one of the girls to cover for me and I ran up there. Our house had a great big hole in the roof and it wasn't much good after that. One of the men told me to take the rest of the night off to sort our stuff out.'

Joan and her mother set to work clearing the wreckage that was left of their house and those of their neighbours.

'Our stuff was everywhere. Mother and I got one of those old tin baths, tied some rope on it, and spent all night lifting it down. We did the two neighbours first, then we did ours. All that rubble in that bath.'

But they managed it, only to encounter a phenomenon that, according to Joan, was a regular occurrence after flying bomb raids. It started to rain.

'It was probably coincidence but it always seemed to happen. There we were, no roof on our house, and it's raining. But the boiler was still going and I said to Mother that I must have a bath. So I did. There was I in the bath with an umbrella up, with Mother standing outside the door with a towel, just in case they came back. Daft really.'

Discomfort and danger became so common, that people almost put it to one side.

Off duty one night, Joan and a friend went to the Davis Theatre in Croydon. They were sitting in the front of the balcony when the building took a direct hit.

'This big bomb came down and, as it came through the roof, it hit the side. I felt it go by, sensed it. It fell down below and killed six people. Lots of other people were hurt. I was so lucky to be alive.'

The experience changed her.

'I was more nervous, much more aware. I remember outside, as they were bringing them out, there was this man. He was dead, but he still had a cigarette alight. You don't forget things like that, do you?'

Joan is now a dog breeder, regularly showing at Crufts. She lives near Hastings.

WOMEN'S VOLUNTARY SERVICE

The WVS was set up in 1938. Staffed by older women, women with childcare commitments, or medical conditions that compromised their fitness for active service, it had over one million members by the end of the war.

Its purpose was to train other women for civil defence work and manage the intrusions into ordinary civilian life. It also managed recycling schemes, ran clothing centres, emergency accommodation, canteens and rest centres. WVS women often accompanied children when they were evacuated, attempting to re-home them as safely and sensitively as possible.

By 1943, the WVS was well-established throughout Britain. In a speech, in which he remarked on their distinctive and womanly contribution to victory, Herbert Morrison, Home Secretary and Minister of Home Security declared:

'These women who, had it not been for their own tireless enthusiasm on one hand and a first class piece of national organisation on the other, might many of them never have been fitted into the pattern of the nation's war effort. Just what a loss that would have been we could now see, when we considered the manifold tasks that the WVS had undertaken.' (The Times 27th April, 1943).

The WVS was later awarded Royal approval and is still an active Society today.

CHAPTER THIRTY ONE

Irene Parnell - WVS

Irene Parnell was too young to enlist or to work in a factory. She was still only sixteen when the war finished, but was determined not to let her age get in the way of contributing to the war effort.

'We lived in the country, not far from Plymouth, and I desperately wanted to do something for the war. I was too young to go into the services, too young to drive, and there wasn't really an opportunity to work in factories or anything near where we lived.'

Irene's mother had started work with the Women's Voluntary Service. As an active member of the church she had always helped out in the community and WVS work seemed to come naturally to her. It was not something that Irene considered for herself.

'I was young and, although it was war, joining up and leaving home all seemed so glamorous. I didn't want to run tea vans and things, I wanted to be up there in the thick of it. But I was too young and it finished too soon for me to get the opportunity.'

Ironically, one of Irene's biggest regrets was her honesty, something that still rankles, even today.

'I've met so many people since the war who told me that they lied about their age to get into things during the war. Do you know, it never occurred to me to do that and I could kick myself now. I never thought to do that - how silly - and I could easily have passed for two years older!'

Instead, after leaving school at fourteen, she worked in an office by day and, in the evenings, joined her mother with her WVS duties. It is only now that she realises the efforts of the WVS were every bit as valuable as any of the other organisations, particularly their work in the rest centres for people who had lost their homes.

'It sounds a bit cheeky to say I wanted to do something else, but I did. But I still made the best of helping my mother. I remember making endless buckets of tea and washing things up - and I didn't like that very much at all. And sorting out the scraps and stuff; it used to be my job to save all the tea leaves and the peelings from all the stuff we cooked. I had to make sure that the right things went into the right buckets and that they didn't get too full. Then somebody would come round and collect it all up and we'd start filling more buckets, not that we wasted much in the first place. It was all stuff that we couldn't use and it all went off to feed the animals. I often used to wonder what wartime animals thought about their diet - they were quite well-fed, albeit on a strange selection of things'.

Despite the events that had led people to the rest centres, Irene remembers the time she spent in them as lively and fun.

'Some people had lost everything - and in some cases, several times. Then there would be people who'd lost people in the bombing or in the fighting abroad, but they still managed to carry on. You hear people talking about the 'Dunkirk spirit' where everybody pulled together. Well, it really was like that - people helped each other out.'

People who had not had anything in common until conflict linked them, would settle down and carry on as if they had known each other for years. They talked endlessly, sang, watched each other's children.

War brings out the best and worst in human nature, but for those less scrupulous, the daily disruption to life offered many opportunities too attractive to ignore.

'I remember this woman whose house had been blasted. It was doors and windows hanging off and that sort of thing. Well, she had two small children, so she'd gone straight to the rest centre, intending to go back and salvage what she could. When she did get back, her place had been looted and she was more upset about that than anything else. I don't think she had much to take - nobody did - but it was the fact that somebody else had taken what little she had was what really upset her.'

On another occasion, somebody was caught trying to sell stolen food.

'Everybody swapped stuff and sold bits and pieces that they had. That was just what they did. But one day, there was a right fuss when a chap came in with some eggs. I don't know how they found out but it turned out that he'd pinched them from somebody's allotment where they had chickens. You just didn't do that sort of thing and he was sorted out by some of the ARP men.'

As she got older, Irene became more involved in WVS

activities and was entrusted with some more exacting tasks - as well as the inevitable tea making.

'When I was about fifteen, I helped to run a mobile canteen that went to railway stations. That was great and I loved it because it was for the soldiers. We were there to make them tea and buns and stuff. Well, you can imagine that - I was fifteen and I had all these soldiers paying me attention. I was a bit shy at first I suppose - and I used to blush, but I still loved it.'

In the meantime, while Irene felt she was, at last, doing something useful, her mother continued to work in the community wherever she was needed.

'Mother had gone on quite a few trips with schools where they'd been evacuated to safer places. She'd go off and come back several days later, having accompanied groups of little children to various places. When she went, I was left with my aunt who would come and live at our house.'

And then there was the unpicking and mending and general saving of anything useful.

'Everybody saved things during the war - we always seemed to have lots of string and paper in bundles at our house. It got collected regularly but I don't really remember it happening. It was just there and then it wasn't. But I do remember mother sitting for hours unpicking jumpers and winding wool.'

WVS women gathered in Irene's home and between them they wrote letters, hundreds of them, to pen pals and their own men overseas.

'My father was in North Africa and Mother and I would write to him. But we also used to write to soldiers and sailors through a pen pal arrangement and I think that was something that the WVS had started up, too. I quite liked doing that, although sometimes it got a bit difficult trying to make each letter interesting. I mean, how many times can you tell somebody about making cups of tea before you get bored with it, let alone them getting fed up? So, one day, my aunt suggested that I wrote about the pictures and film stars. So that's what I did. I wrote about films I'd seen and actors that I admired.'

When the war came to an end, WVS work seemed to be more in demand than ever. As the men and women who had been posted overseas returned to Britain, they swelled the numbers of those already living with what was left of the shattered country.

'It was quite odd, really. The fighting had stopped and I suppose you'd think things would go back to normal. But it took time. Of course, houses had gone, factories and places where people had worked had been blown up, and there were places you couldn't go because of dangerous structures or unexploded bombs. Everything was all in a right muddle. So the WVS went on feeding people and finding them places to stay, and getting them clothes to replace stuff they'd lost. And rationing went on for years.'

Only later, after the war ended, did the real impact of the WVS emerge. Although their efforts were recognised during those long years, it was those they had helped who ensured their efforts were put into perspective. Men who had had their socks made or mended by WVS women, soldiers who had received letters from pen pals, or people who had been helped by a volunteer when they really needed it. These are the people who bore testimony to the tireless care and service these women gave.

While Irene Parnell might have considered her job less than stimulating, she was part of something that helped keep the country going and was vital to its survival. As Herbert Morrison reported in The Times newspaper (27th April 1943):

'It was something that no man could do and something that the whole nation would not forget. We could see their good works. We could see them in every town, in almost every village street.'

AIR RAID PRECAUTIONS

Plans to manage the expected devastation of the big towns and cities across the country had been worked out before war started. Various people in each community were appointed Air Raid Precaution Wardens, or ARPs as they became known. Tasked with logging the personal details of local people, the information proved invaluable when bodies had to be identified, searches initiated for those missing, or for notifying next of kin. Women ARP staff were particularly useful as they knew which child belonged to which parent, who lived where and how many people comprised each household.

Wardens also ran the shelters, gave people advice on who to ask for replacement clothes, which buildings were safe and how to ensure black out regulations were fully complied with. They helped direct rescue work once the 'all-clear' had sounded, assessed the extent of the damage, and the response needed. They tended the injured, helped them to safety, and cared for them if friends or family had been killed.

Wardens called at addresses where light was visible, and reported those who flouted regulations. It was, therefore, exceptionally embarrassing when one of their own was caught disregarding the regulations. When

Charles Ellis, a Warden from Croydon, left a light showing from the top of his shop, he was relieved of ten pounds by the Croydon Bench. (Croydon Advertiser, 28.8.1940)

Occasionally, they saved an offender from public hostility. When a crowd of fifty angry people besieged a house showing a light in Thornton Heath, Surrey, the occupant was rescued by an ARP warden. The tenant was later fined five pounds for his error. (Croydon Advertiser, August 28th 1940).

Many ARP wardens were also affected by the bombing. One woman ARP ambulance driver, ferrying casualties after a particularly heavy night-time raid, remained on duty after her own home was bombed and her family buried in the debris. She later received a commendation for her courage and dedication. (Croydon Advertiser, 28.8.40)

Air Raid Precaution work, like many other wartime occupations, was dangerous. Falling debris, shrapnel, fires, secondary explosions and flying glass all took their toll. Many wardens, men and women, died trying to help others.

CHAPTER THIRTY TWO

Winnie Viner - ARP and Nurse

At the beginning of the war, Winnie Viner was waiting to get married. Her fiancé was a sailor in the regular Navy, while Winnie worked as a nurse. They were both twenty-three.

'Vice and I got married in 1940 and we were quite lucky because we had a big room in my mother's house in Dorking. It was a large house, so we had our own space and it was our own home.'

In those early days Winnie was still nursing at Camberwell Hospital in South London but when it was bombed, she was evacuated with half the hospital staff to Dartford in Kent.

'I didn't like it at Dartford. I was a general nurse and I didn't like the hospital. The final straw came for me when they sent me to theatre. When we had the first batch of casualties come in they were sailors from the North Sea convoys. They were all injured and they were also smothered in oil and tar. It used to really upset me because Vic was on those convoys and I couldn't take it.'

It upset her so much that she resigned.

She returned to Surrey and spent some time working as a nurse in Dorking Hospital where she was put in charge of a ward. By 1940, the old Police Station in the High Street in Dorking was being used as an Air Raid Precaution Centre. Winnie knew the person in charge and decided to direct her war effort there.

'I really wanted to do something and I was very determined. When I worked at the Centre I had to take messages about aircraft coming our way. We used to get calls from the Royal Observer Corps women and they'd tell us what to expect. That information had to go to the controller so that we could work out positions and where the bombs would be likely to fall. We set the sirens off once we knew all of that.'

Whilst the ARP Centre in Dorking may not have been in the thick of the bombing, it was still an important part of the defence network. During raids, Winnie watched the waves of aircraft.

'We had a lot of children from London billeted in Dorking and when these planes were going over us on their way to drop more bombs on London, I used to wonder how the families of the evacuated children were. Were they killed or injured, would they survive and, when it was all over, would they have any homes to return to?'

Even in rural areas, it was difficult to escape the effects of war.

'A bomb dropped at Westcott nearby and landed on a farm. It exploded and knocked a cottage out but nobody was home at the time. Then there were a lot of incendiaries and so lots of fire.'

Of those injured, many survived and recovered. But those who suffered burns, bore the scars for the rest of their lives.

'There was a young chap who was in the National Fire Service. He'd got badly burned and I remember how disfigured he was. His face was burnt off right up into his hair and his hands were gnarled up. He spent a long time at the burns place at East Grinstead but then he went back into the Fire Service again - taking messages. Vic was at sea all this time and, fortunately, he came back safely and undamaged.'

Life in the ARP post was very busy. Both men and women worked there on shifts round the clock, plotting aircraft and mobilising responses to their actions. For Winnie, it was a method of distraction as well as a way of helping out.

'Vic was away and you never knew. But it was so busy at the ARP post that you didn't have time to sit and think about what might go wrong. It was very hectic; four of us worked on each shift and we took turns at all the duties so we were kept busy all night. It was a happy time, although there was a war on. I had no children to worry about at that time.'

Her mother's house in Rothes Road, Dorking, was also put to good use. The family took in five evacuees who had been bombed out in London.

'They were Sisters from Crossways Central Mission at the Elephant and Castle. When the Mission got hit, they were homeless, so they stayed with my mother until they found alternative accommodation. A friend had also been bombed out. She stayed longer and my husband eventually gave her away when she got married.'

Winnie still lives in Dorking.

CHAPTER THIRTY THREE

Molly Hutchins - Fire Watcher

'I remember how the sky glowed. It was all orange and red and it looked like somebody had turned on great big spotlights over the whole city. But it was London on fire. I shall always remember it as long as I live.'

Molly Hutchins lived in south London, on a ridge of hills that slope down to the London Basin. Some years earlier, in 1936, the sky had been similarly lit up when the Crystal Palace had burnt down. Molly had seen that fire, too, but the fires of London and the docks were something else.

'I remember when the Palace went up and it being a really big event, but seeing the whole of London on fire was breathtaking. Of course, it was war, so that made a big difference, but because we were detached, but also connected with it, it made a big impression on me. I remember thinking, "My God, there are people I know in all that fire." It was stunning.'

Molly worked in an office not far from London Bridge. She was nearly twenty when she first saw the London docks bombed. By that time she was already beginning to get used to the daily and nightly terror that war delivered. Although she was aware of the dangers, she had gone beyond being frightened and was quite fatalistic about life in general. It was this fatalism that made her volunteer as a fire watcher.

'It was a funny feeling. We knew it was dangerous and that we could have gone back home but somehow that didn't seem right. Nothing heroic or anything but it somehow made you feel that as long as you were doing something, then, if you got killed, you'd gone down fighting.'

The need to fight back has been well-documented and ably explains the extraordinary number of people who volunteered their services on the home front. Fire watching was one of the most dangerous.

'They asked for volunteers to go on a rota. It meant you had to stay at work and sleep in the office and my friend and I volunteered. The raids were mostly at night when it was dark, so as we didn't need to go home, we'd nip into the West End for a couple of hours and then come back ready for our fire watching.'

When it was her turn on the rota, Molly slept fully clothed on the bed provided. When the siren went, she donned her tin hat and ran to the ground floor.

'If the sirens went, you either had to go up on the roof and watch where the fires were breaking out, or you had to go to the rendezvous then go out onto the streets to help extinguish any smaller fires. My turn for fire watching came round about every two weeks I think.'

Protection was minimal.

'Well, we had our tin hats and gas masks and we'd wait. Sometimes we waited all night and there was nothing for us to do. Sometimes we'd get sent out straight away to help with the stirrups or to report fires, or deal with incendiaries.'

Apart from the falling bombs and gunfire, there was the ever-present danger of shrapnel and falling masonry.

'We were used to noise generally but during a raid it was deafening. There were bangs and rattles and crashes - you were constantly jumping. And then there was the shrapnel falling out of the sky - which rattled and tinkled. It was all very noisy.'

But, according to Molly, doing something was infinitely better than doing nothing at all.

'Being able to see what was going on wasn't as scary as sitting in a shelter and waiting for something to happen. I had this attitude that if I was going to get killed, that was it. I didn't take unnecessary risks, mind, but I was fed up with the Germans running my life, so being able to see what was going on was good for me.'

Molly and her fellow fire-watchers spent many nights on duty but they were still expected to turn up for work in the morning.

'The ironic thing was, I always woke up if there wasn't an air-raid. It's that feeling of, "It's quiet, what's wrong?" I suppose it was the subconscious anticipation. But then we had really busy nights and it got even worse when the buzz bombs started.'

The flying bombs were noisy, unpredictable and devastating. With their sudden engine cut-out, it was impossible to guess where they would land.,

'With planes, you could tell if they were coming your way, even when our fighters started to chase them and you'd see the searchlights picking out planes in the sky. But the buzz bombs changed direction and glided and suddenly dropped out of the sky. You just couldn't tell where they were going to drop. They were horrible.'

Unable to predict specific danger, the fire watchers' work became more and more uncertain.

'What I didn't like was the not knowing. When you're doing something that's dangerous - and fire watching was - you still worked out how to deal with the unexpected if it happened. And you did that by weighing-up what was going on and where it was happening. But you couldn't do that with the buzz bombs and for me that was almost as bad as sitting in the shelters and waiting for the Germans to attack.'

Molly now lives in New Zealand.

CHAPTER THIRTY FOUR

Nancy Denman - Scrap Collector

'I can't remember now how I got involved in the first place, but I seemed to spend the whole war collecting things for the war effort. If it wasn't bottle caps, it was paper or string or peelings for somebody's bloody chickens.'

Nancy Denman was twenty-two when the war started and she had a small son. As a young mother she wasn't called up to do war work but she still found a way of contributing. One of four sisters from Coventry, her war had begun with tragedy.

'My husband was a regular soldier so he'd gone off to France as soon as it all started. He got caught up in the Dunkirk business and was captured, but then he died. He got injured and didn't recover, so that was it. He was twenty six and the baby was eighteen months old.'

As a single parent, Nancy could have faced a very difficult future. But her close working class family helped her to deal with her husband's death and get back on her feet.

'We all looked after each other anyway and all lived close by. So when Eddie died, it just sort of happened and that was that. In a way, I was fortunate that he got killed straight off - not that I wanted him to die, of course, but you see I didn't have the worry that other people had. Once he was gone, he was gone, and I just had to accept it and look after my baby. Some poor people had to worry about their men for six years only for them to get killed at the end, or to be badly injured.'

Nancy began to look after her sisters' children and then became their unofficial childminder, with the occasional local child added in for good measure. It meant that she had some income and was able to look after her own son. She also felt she was doing something useful.

'They'd give me a bit for looking after the children and we all shared rations anyway, so it worked out quite well. They knew the children were safe with me. I'd take them out and it kept my mind off things, too. It helped them out.'

It also gave her the opportunity to get out and about and, eventually, this developed into salvage work.

'We had a couple of allotments and I used to take the children up there in the summer. It was also a good place to pile up all the stuff we were supposed to collect - old lids and paper, bottle tops, bits of metal. It was out of the way and there was loads of room.'

Before long, Nancy got a name for scavenging. Wartime campaigns such as ' Dig for Victory', 'Wings for Victory' and 'Every little bit helps' had become ingrained in the Nation's psyche and many people viewed it as a real way of helping the war effort.

Some of her neighbours took things straight to her allotment, others to her house. She then sorted it into piles, tied it together and handed it over to the man who collected it.

'We used to call it 'treasure' and the children loved going round collecting it all up. We called it 'the treasure hunt' and we'd spend all day doing that. I had a little cart that somebody made me - just a handcart thing, and I'd wheel it round and fill it up with bits and pieces as I went.'

Then Nancy moved up a gear. She got into swill.

'Various people kept chickens and rabbits and they always needed peelings to feed them. I can't remember who started it but, before long, I was going round with a couple of old tin buckets and an old dustbin in my little cart, collecting peelings and the scraps from the houses.'

She then re-distributed her hoard between the chicken and rabbit- keepers in exchange for eggs or the occasional rabbit.

'I kept a book so it was all fair and I'd mark down who'd given how much and they'd get the most eggs, or the biggest rabbit, or whatever. Then more and more people wanted to join in and it got a bit much, so I had to just stick to our street and a couple of streets nearby.'

As well as helping in the Nation's bid to make the best use of materials, re-cycling made it a little easier for those whose homes had been bombed or blasted. With their possessions destroyed and their homes in various stages of collapse, many found it easier to live with fewer things.

'The more you had, the more you missed it if it all went wrong. You see, none of us had much in those days and there wasn't this thing about having the latest this or the biggest that. If you got bombed, you got bombed and we were all the same. But clearing up was somehow that little bit more bearable if you knew that what the Germans had broken, you were giving to the war effort and having a go back indirectly. It was quite funny in a way to think that your broken saucepan might be made into the bomb that eventually got Hitler.'

Nancy has no idea how much scrap she collected over five years or how many rabbits and chickens she fattened up in the name of freedom. But she does know that it was more than the average household.

'It started off as something to keep me occupied really but then it turned into quite an operation. But it was good for me as it was a difficult time and I felt that, by the end of it, I'd somehow done all right by Eddie.'

Nancy married again after the war and now lives near Birmingham.

CHAPTER THIRTY FIVE

Margaret Cornish - Canals

Whilst the war touched most of Britain, especially in the more urban areas, there were parts of society that carried on with their usual way of life, seemingly without reference to, or acknowledgement of, the fighting and disruption.

These groups maintained an odd position, often working closely within the community, yet at the same time keeping their distance. They were the canal boat people.

Canals linked most parts of Britain and were still used to transport bulky materials. Even in the 1940's the network, often dubbed the motorways of the nineteenth century, was still a working communication system.

With the disruption that war brought, the canals once again offered an alternative, albeit slower method of moving materials. Criss-crossing the countryside as they did, unlit and unnoticed, the canals were rarely a target for German attention. The overriding impediment to their use was that many boaters had already left the waterways for life ashore, leaving boats moored but crewless.

Margaret Cornish was a teacher. She had grown up in Devon in a time when money and status still paved the way to success. However, as a gifted but financially poor student, with a dislike of privilege and rite, she had begun to carve out an individual life for herself.

'I was a loner and I liked walking and sailing. In later times, I would have been a hippie or a New Age traveller but back then I was a teacher but not a very happy one. I was constantly looking for the right peg to fit into the right hole.'

Yet all she seemed to find were more and more wrong pegs. The turning point came when she received a telegram advising her that, as a teacher, she would be evacuated.

'It meant I would have to go to an unknown destination. That didn't worry me but then I discovered that I would not be evacuated with the children that I was teaching. And, of course, that made a big difference.'

She resigned her teaching post and considered what she might do. A friend brought an advertisement to her attention. The Ministry of Transport were looking for women to crew canal boats. This was Margaret's right peg; she applied and was taken on immediately.

'My lifestyle had been around boats for years and I'd always sailed. Being a loner and liking a basic lifestyle, it was easy for me to fit in and the life suited me. But the scheme wasn't very widely advertised so it didn't become that well known.'

To an outsider the boating life appeared calm and leisurely. The reality was very different. Every part of it was determined by an ability to operate locks, maintain an engine, steer a course and get to a destination as quickly as possible. It was physically demanding, needing strength and agility. Margaret was at home immediately but many of her companions had a hard time getting used to it.

'I suppose it seemed a romantic existence, but it had grim undertones. It was very hard and there was no rest time or comforts. We only had a bucket as a toilet and we worked all the time. We were always wet, dirty and on our own, living in a very cramped space. We were quite a motley lot but there was a very strong bond that grew between us.'

Many boating families were unhappy about what they regarded as the intrusion of outsiders into their world.

'These people lived totally on the canals. They had grown up on the water and everything was centred on it. They really didn't want us there, getting in their way and being in their world. And in a way, although we were novices, we were competition for cargo, and it bred resentment.'

But the women were there to stay, a representation of the wider world, although in reality there was only a core of about twenty trainees who endured the harsh conditions and finally earned acceptance. Turnover was high but, surprisingly, those who stayed were the women who, on the surface, would perhaps have been least likely to do so.

'Many of us who stayed came from middle-class backgrounds and not from the working class, although some who did were very good. I think it was a combination of various things and differences in upbringing. Many had been Girl Guides and had a taste for the outside life, and they hadn't got the extended family ties that some women had. So I suppose they were used to being more on their own and not part of a system where they would miss people, or have to fit into a particular place in their family network.'

Ironically, the boating families themselves had very strong traditions which were more akin to the novices who left.

'The whole family worked together and helped each other out. They were very traditional and the women boaters didn't wear trousers and thought us very odd for doing so. They all wore long skirts and each boat was a separate entity, although they were all part of the boater community.'

Each family worked for itself and, in a sense, the women crews became a group in their own right, all pulling together to survive, doing their job and delivering their cargo. But, as outsiders, the task was hard.

'The boaters had real expertise from years of doing it, and the skills were passed down the generations. It was impossible to learn these things quickly, so we had to do our best and cultivate contacts as we went. We also had to find food along the way, as well as other essential supplies, especially women's things, such as sanitary products.'

There was no way of learning from other sources. No manuals, plans or diagrams to help the novice crews.

They were an itinerant people who were rarely educated and mostly illiterate. With nothing written down, everything was passed on by word of mouth. Whilst Margaret and her colleagues could learn a certain amount by watching and by trial and error, they knew that the only way to really learn was to earn their acceptance.

'There were two families who gradually did - the Smiths and the Sibleys, but we had to prove ourselves and they only accepted those of us who stayed and worked at it.

The canal people were fiercely independent and were viewed as riff-raff by shore people, so it's no wonder they were so withdrawn.'

However, a sign that Margaret had met with their approval and been sanctioned, came one Christmas when she was invited into a boater's cabin.

'This was a great privilege. Lil Smith invited me in. She had spent some time ashore with her grandmother at Braunston. Somewhere, Lil had learned to read, which was very unusual, and she read to us that Christmas from "A Christmas Carol."

The women worked in crews of three, running two boats. The boat in front pulled the other in a boat/barge arrangement. Their cargo varied from trip to trip; sometimes it was cement, sometimes steel, more often it was coal.

'We'd be loaded at the start and unloaded at the finish of the trip but we still had to manage the cargo en route. Sometimes we had to shift it in the hold to level out the boat and, sometimes, if something went wrong with the bilge, we had to move it to keep it dry. You can imagine how filthy we were and we had no washing facilities.'

They also had to maintain their own engine, only seeking help if absolutely necessary. Running repairs, makeshift alterations and daily adjustments all became part of Margaret's life. And then there were the locks. It was not simply a matter of operating them, but observing the canal etiquette.

'Everything was a race against time, although it looked very peaceful and sedate to an outsider. We had to take it in turns to wheel locks and that meant cycling ahead to prepare the locks for the boat to go straight in and then make it ready for the next boat. Then you'd go onto the next one and the next one.'

Etiquette came in the form of knowing who had priority if two boats arrived close together, where to tie-up and what was expected in terms of helping other boats through.

'They'd try it on but you had to try not to let them get the better of you, and without causing an argument. Whoever was in the right, we women were always the outsiders and in the small world of canals, enemies were dangerous to have.'

There was much to be learned but they were given initial training - on the job. It was conducted by one of two women outsiders at the heart of the transport scheme: Daphne or Kit. Margaret was trained by Daphne.

'You were either one of Kit's girls or one of Daphne's. Daphne was very tolerant, very independent and I liked her. She had been in the ATS but had then gone on the canals. I worked with her a lot. Kit had been a ballet teacher before the war - a very good one. As a result, she was very up front, very strong, although she was very small.'

Both trainers managed to keep tabs on their recruits through the water based contact system. Margaret recalled that it worked, even though there was no electricity, no formal news, radio nor any real established means of communication. Information was passed from boat to boat and between boat to shore, but only if those with the information wanted to pass it on.

'It was a wonderful narrow ribbon of people who

connected with other people but did not belong anywhere in particular. They were a separate entity living within the rest of the community.

However tenuous it had become, many of the women still maintained a land link. Margaret's flat in London had been hit by a V1 but her now detached lifestyle meant that, although she worked very hard, she also lived relatively cheaply. This enabled her to pay for a room in Elm Park Gardens, Chelsea, out of her boat wages.

'It cost me ten shillings a week and we were paid about three pounds a week I think, so I could afford to keep it on. But going home on leave became very symbolic for me. There was this definite feeling that when I stepped on and off the boat, I was stepping into and out of my two worlds.'

For Margaret, her home was now the water. Already distanced from her family before the war had started, life on the canals had given her the independence she craved.

'After a while, I realised how removed I had become. I realised that people whom I thought I knew and that were part of my shore life were often really just people that were there and that I didn't really want to know. I just didn't fit into that neat little arrangement.'

As Margaret passed up and down the country, the war carried on, rarely affecting her specifically, but still attracting her attention.

'I remember passing through Coventry and it was all but demolished. Then there were waterside factories that were hit from time to time and we'd see flames and all sorts of activity. Limehouse in London was at the end of most trips. This is where we had to unload and reload. It was a big pond at the heart of the dock area and we were always in a hurry to get away because it was a real target all of the time. We were very lucky and always managed to escape.'

Her cargo, once discharged, meant that Margaret could depart once more.

'The canals were mostly deserted and even the towpaths were in disrepair; we rarely saw anybody other than boaters. But when we got to London, we were twenty feet down on the water and you had to climb up the ladder. It was like coming up into another world, a busy world. Then we went out the same way as we left. It was a very peculiar feeling.'

After two and a half years Margaret's life on the water came to an end in May 1945. The news that hostilities had ceased seemed almost incidental.

'We were being loaded - with coal, I think. The chap shouted the news down to us but none of us stopped what we were doing. We just sort of said, "Oh" and carried on, loaded up and we were away. Life on the boats even then never really was part of mainstream life.'

Margaret now lives in Suffolk. Her boat, 'Hyperion', is working the canals once more in The Midlands.

CHAPTER THIRTY SIX

Margaret McFarlane - Entertainer

Over the years, The Brownies have been the making of many girls but for a nine year-old Firefly, it was the start of a wartime theatrical career that would take her from her home town in Scotland to some of the best known stages of Britain.

'I was in The Brownies and I was in a big display in the town hall in Paisley. So was our Frances. She was three years older than me. I was in the Firefly Six and I was dead proud. It was the first time that I'd been in a show or done anything like that, and I loved it. So, that was me hooked.'

Margaret McFarlane was the youngest of three girls, each conveniently spaced three years apart. Neither of her parents had a theatrical background, nor any ambitions in that direction.

'Nobody pushed us or made us do it but because I'd enjoyed it so much, when we came off stage Mother said she'd get us into dancing lessons. At the time, they cost one and six a lesson, so there was to be no mucking about. I learned national dancing and my sister specialised in tap dancing and ballet.'

Although it was Margaret's ambition to go on the stage,

she was still only a child and school came first. Frances, three years older and harbouring the same ambition, was biding her time until her younger sister was able to leave school and form a double-act with her.

The age for leaving school was fourteen but by the time Margaret reached thirteen and a half, the war had started. Opportunities to entertain the troops began to emerge. For Margaret this was a godsend.

'It meant we got going very quickly. We were always out and about singing here and dancing there, and entertaining anyway, but this was even better.'

It would be inconceivable today to cast two young girls into the world of show business without at least a manager to look out for them. The McFarlane sisters were protected by their own and their parents' naivety. Without prior knowledge of the world of entertainment, it was a case of 'what you don't know won't harm you.'

'There were some parents who kept on at their children and really pushed them, but our parents didn't. Mother used to make our outfits and she was dead proud, but they never made us go to places just so we could get famous. As I remember it, we just did it ourselves and we never thought of ourselves as anything different. I mean, we were just two wee lassies who liked to dance and sing and we were thrilled that folk actually wanted to listen to us and seemed to like us. It was great.'

With six months to go before she could leave school, Margaret made her own contribution to the war effort.

'I made pyjamas for the soldiers. Paisley was a cotton town and we had a mill that turned out bales. Our school had three sewing machines - an electric one, a hand machine, and one of those treadle contraptions. So that's what we did. We made pyjamas for the soldiers.'

When her six months were up both the sisters began their career.

'Captain McCulloch was the husband of Kathy Kay - she was a singer with the Billy Cotton Band. We started to work for the Captain on a semi-professional basis, going round all the ack-ack batteries in the Glasgow area and singing there, entertaining.'

Their first show, prior to going professional, was compered by a woman who, according to Margaret, was serving in the ATS and was hoping to get into ENSA - the Entertainment National Service Association.

'The woman that did the compering was Janet Brown. She wasn't known then. She wasn't a member of ENSA then, either. I remember we bumped into her one day in Sauchiehall Street in Glasgow, me and Frances. She stopped us and asked us how she could get in.'

ENSA became the focal point of show business in Britain during the war years. It provided entertainment for the troops and those engaged in war work. Many well-known entertainers either started off working with ENSA as civilians, or were seconded to it from the services. Others got their first break there, eventually emerging from a service background to the professional stage.

The association was professionally run, with performers required to pass an audition. Margaret and Frances went to the Theatre Royal in Glasgow to be seen by the agent Horace Collins. He liked what he saw and they began touring. Now called The Max Sisters, by the standards of the day, they were well-paid.

'I was not yet fifteen, me, and our fee for the act was ten pounds. That doesn't sound a lot nowadays, but it was more than a man's wage. And there we were, two wee lassies, singing and dancing because we liked it. Great!'

The sisters travelled throughout Scotland and England with the five handed shows they were signed to.

'We were getting to see all sorts of places and we travelled in great luxury - in a Black Maria! The three men that were in the show rode in the front while Frances and I were bundled into the back.'

It now seems unthinkable that two young girls could roam the length and breadth of Britain in the company of three men they hardly knew.

'We didn't need chaperones because we were of age and we were signed professionally. We just went to shows and the five of us were all part of it. Mind you, the men did like their drink and they'd go into a pub and leave Frances and me in the van. It was so cold out there I remember.'

Every now and again, they rebelled against such treatment. On one occasion, Frances decided to put a stop to the pub and van arrangement.

'Our Frances decided she'd had enough. I can see her now, her nose was turning green with cold and she was all fluffed up. So out she went, into the pub and said to the men that if they didn't come out right then, she'd tell somebody how they were treating us. But one of them said to her, "Listen lassie, you've only been in the business for two minutes, so you be quiet and not be having so much to say."'

The men continued drinking between shows and The Max Sisters stayed in the van. Then, one memorable day, they got their revenge.

'We were on stage, doing our act, dancing away and the part came for us to stop and the music should have started. But there was complete silence. When I l looked round to see what had happened, the pianist was sound asleep. He'd had a wee drink too many and nodded off.'

As the months went by, The Max Sisters graduated to better and bigger shows.

'We did three after that. We were in "More Heather Breezes", "Scotch Broth" and "Double Scotch". There was a mixture of Scottish people and English people in those and we took the show right up to the Shetlands and down to Portsmouth, entertaining in real theatres. I loved it.'

While they were based in the Shetland Isles, they were entertained after the show on a submarine.

'We all went on board and they were drinking. I wasn't. I was only about fifteen anyway, but this stuff seemed really strong and the crew and the cast were knocking it back. Their eyes seemed to be bulging. But when we were leaving, we were coming down the gangplank and one of the girls was so plastered that she slipped off and nearly fell into the water. Fortunately, even though she was the worse for wear, she managed to save herself. She was a contortionist and she wrapped her legs around the plank and hung there. I can still see her now!'

After the Shetland Isles, they moved back down through Scotland to Inverness where they lived in a castle, just outside Beauly.

'We stayed in some beautiful places, but we were young and, looking back, I don't think we appreciated it at the time, although we did have fun. That castle was something else and we'd be in our beds at night and we'd hear chains rattling and ghostly noises. It was some of the men in the show playing about, but we'd nearly jump out of our skins! Then there was another place where there was a big church organ thing and the men would go up there and pump air into it to make spooky sounds, and then we'd have seances in some of these places.'

The isolation and the beauty of the Scottish Highlands was similarly lost on The Max Sisters. It did, however, provide the chance to buy eggs and produce from nearby farms to take back to their mother in Paisley.

'We decided to go up the Gareloch - walking, of course, and intending to find farms. It was like I'd imagine Canada to be - all mountains and trees and lochs. As we went up to one farm, we could hear all this music and noise. We got closer and an American sailor came out. It turned out that there were about twelve of them there and they'd taken over a house. Their ship was in the Gareloch, hidden up. It was a place that we found out the ships on the North Atlantic used to rest up as it was a sheltered hiding place from the U boats and that. So we had a great time that day - twelve American sailors all to ourselves, and we sang and danced and had a grand old time!'

Despite their success, The Max Sisters remained unaffected by their popularity.

'My Mother made all of our costumes and we were always well turned out. I don't know where she got the material mind. And she'd bought us each a pair of kidskin dancing shoes, silver they were, with tie-up fronts. They'd cost her three guineas each and that was serious money in those days. Once, we put them on top of a stove when we lived in very cold digs and the heat made them curl up. Luckily, we noticed in time, we wouldn't have been able to get a new pair.'

Their mother continued making their outfits until they finally achieved recognition nationwide.

'We were at the Theatre Royal in Drury Lane and Sir Cecil Hardwicke walked in. He looked us up and down and sort of sneered at our outfits. I remember looking at him and thinking, "You're a poor fellow, you are, looking at me like you are something special," and then he sent us backstage to pick out some dresses. We picked two beautiful pale blue organza dresses for the finale and two more for the opening. They were so sophisticated and we were anything but, but the important thing was that we could sing and dance. I can still remember how he looked at us, and we picked out the dresses because he was so snooty. We thought we'd use them and save poor old Mum.'

Margaret and Frances never forgot that their audiences were working in areas that were not only dangerous, but vital if the war against Germany was to be won. If their act could help the troops forget their worries for even an hour, then they felt they were contributing.

'I didn't really have a favourite theatre or anything and I was never one for this business of thinking I was somebody because I'd been on a stage somewhere famous. What I loved best was going round to the camps and doing the shows there. I think it was because we were entertaining the people who were going out fighting and risking their lives for us. It was always special to do a show for them because we felt we owed them really.'

But there was sadness, too. As Margaret knew, these men and women were at the front line of the war - and sometimes it affected them directly.

'We were always well entertained ourselves after a show and on one occasion we were in Yorkshire. There were a lot of RAF camps there, and we'd done the show and were having a drink but the lads seemed different. They were over-jolly and seemed to be trying really hard. I asked one of the boys what was happening and said that they seemed different. He told me that that's what they did when they'd lost a colleague - it was their way of coping with a death. Then he told me that one of their boys was lying dead in the next room having been killed when his plane blew up when it landed. It was their way of celebrating his life. But it was sad.'

A few months later, death came close again.

'We'd done this show and were being entertained afterwards and I remember that there were six big New Zealand boys there. They were pilots and I remember that their uniforms were that khaki colour. They came and said how much they'd enjoyed the show and asked us where we were playing the next night. They were smashing fellas and they said they would come and see us the next night. But they never turned up. I remember thinking, "Fair enough, if that's how you feel", but then I found out that they'd been on a raid that night after we'd left and none of them had come back.'

Although death became an everyday occurrence, it still came as a shock.

Margaret had many pen friends during the war and found it hard to deal with when she discovered that one of them had died.

'It used to get me every time. I'd realise that I hadn't heard from one of them for a while. Sometimes I would hear eventually and, I suppose, some of them just stopped writing. But some of them stopped because they were dead, and it took a while for that to dawn on me. An Australian friend of mine was killed in the last days of the war. He was one of the very last and that was really sad. All that time he'd been fighting and then he gets killed right at the end. Terrible.'

Margaret had met a pilot during the war and, in August 1945, she married him. Although the fighting was over, the country now had to be rebuilt. The demand for entertainment continued and even in the week of her wedding, Margaret was asked to go back on the stage.

'I'd only been married a few days and I had a call saying that they wanted to put on a big show for the Navy, and would I do it? Well, of course I would, but it wasn't the best of timing. So they said that I could bring my wedding guests to the show. Well, that was very unusual, they wouldn't normally have outsiders there, for insurance purposes. If something happened, then that would be a problem. But they did on this occasion and we all trooped off to the show and Frances and I did our stuff.'

Margaret's new husband had little interest in the theatre, and did not want his wife to continue her career.

'We had a female singer who did solos. We called them 'sobriquets' in those days. Anyway, she stopped what she was doing after one number and said that I had just got married and that my husband was in the audience. Then she dedicated her next song to us, "It had to be you."

Well, I could see him sinking further and further down in his seat. He hated that!'

With a new phase of her life about to begin, Margaret prepared for married life. On reflection, she wonders what might have become of The Max Sisters.

'We were good, Frances and me. We had a great time and we loved it. But in those days it was expected that once you were married, you'd give up your career. It's only recently that I've thought about what I could have done and got annoyed about it. I'm not bitter, mind, but I do wonder what I could have done if attitudes were different back then.'

Sadly, Frances died in an accident when she was just fifty. Margaret lives near Hampton Court in Middlesex.

CHAPTER THIRTY SEVEN

Audrey Boyd - Bus Conductress

'I was a clippie in Birmingham for a while and I loved it. It was hard work but it was good fun, too, especially if, like me, you liked a good old chat. And I thought it was dead glamorous.'

Life on the buses during the war was prone to being rather precarious, even when the German planes were engaged elsewhere.

'Well, the roads were full of potholes and there was always something in the way that had fallen off a building, or was part of a barrier or something. You got used to it, wiggling down the road rather than going in a straight line, but I soon learned to stand on the back platform without even having to hold on!'

Audrey Boyd was employed by the Midland Red Bus Company in Birmingham, a step up from her previous job.

'I worked in a canteen not far from the garage and I liked that, too. The drivers came in and always pulled your leg about something. But I got a bit bored just cooking and clearing up, and decided that I would join them on the buses.'

Although she enjoyed it, she found the work more demanding than she had anticipated.

'I soon found out that it was more than doing tickets, dinging the bell and chatting to the passengers. You had to keep tally of everything as you went - and that meant adding up in your head as you went along. And I'd be up and down those stairs, trying to hang on for dear life but also trying to look as if I wasn't flustered.'

The bus network in Britain was vital to the war effort. With petrol rationed and very few people having access to a car, for many it was the only means of getting about. Some journeys were more eventful than others.

'The blackout was the worst. The windows were all taped up so you couldn't see out and there were no streetlights or headlamps. Although we didn't go that fast, we often used to have near misses. Either something in the road or somebody walking out in front of us, or us nearly driving into something.'

In the early stages of the blackout, very little lighting was allowed and the number of road accidents increased dramatically. The Government was forced take action in a bid to reduce the casualty rate.

Life as a conductress could be quite demanding when an air-raid started. Far from panic, many people declined to be inconvenienced and refused to get off the bus. This made Audrey's task of persuading them into shelters more than difficult.

'When the sirens started, I used to wonder if the Germans could see my bus, and if they could, were they about to home in on it? I mean it was a great big thing that wasn't easy to hide, was it? But it was the passengers that came first, and we'd been trained to deal with them before anything else. Some would get off right away, others - especially the men from the works - would egg each other on and try and appear the least worried.'

Knowing what to do and when to do it was all part of her job. Her passengers, however, often had other ideas.

'We'd been trained to keep going until it was too dangerous to carry on. We had to decide when that was and then we had to get everybody off in a hurry. Once the driver had decided it was getting a bit too close, they'd head for the nearest shelter and it was my job to get them all off without a rush. Only some people who were quite near their homes didn't want to get off. I used to shout at them, "Get off my bloody bus and down the bloody shelter!" That usually worked.'

One of the things Audrey found difficult to deal with was the break in the middle of the day. Whilst it was pleasant to have a rest, it made the return to work even harder.

'They stopped running so many during the day to save petrol but, of course, it meant that towards the end of the day there were even more people wanting to get on fewer buses and I was run off my feet. And what with all the adding up and the tickets and that, I was always shattered by home time.'

The winter months were hard for the bus crews. As the nights drew in, people left work earlier to be sure to get home before the raids started.

'Even during the war, people liked to walk more in the summer. But come the autumn and winter, nobody wanted to be outside in the cold. Mind you, I was never cold - I ran up and down those stairs so often that I was in a permanent sweat.'

While Audrey enjoyed talking to people, the job description, 'Always be cheerful and friendly' could be quite a strain. Sometimes she longed for just a little time to herself, even if only to keep her books.

'I think its one of those jobs. You have to be the smiling face or the cheery soul even when you're tired or fed up or just plain grumpy. I loved being a clippie and most of the time I could do the chat and the singing and all that. But I'd always been one to move on, and I decided that I'd quite like to do something else after a couple of years. So I joined the ATS as a driver.'

Audrey emigrated to Australia after the war, where she worked in a Sydney Zip fastener factory. She now lives in Warwickshire.

CHAPTER THIRTY EIGHT

Vera Manley - Air Ministry Typist

Vera Manley worked in Woolworth's in Henley-on-Thames during the early war years. It was a regular shop job and not terribly inspiring. Then she met a man who changed her life.

'He was a just a man in the Labour Exchange and he asked what my typing was like. I told him that it wasn't all that, but he said that I would do and would I like to go and work for him?'

Her new employer worked with the Royal Air Force Central Examinations Board.

'They told me it was secret work from the start. There was a big house in Sherlock Road near Twyford and the RAF had requisitioned it. That was where the RAF officers sat their exams. Well, you can imagine, there was the big hall of this really grand house filled up with RAF men - and me who couldn't type. I couldn't imagine what they wanted me to do!'

Vera was needed to type examination results and various records.

'When I arrived at the house, I was picked up by this camouflaged car and driven from Twyford station to the house. That was funny in itself - I'd always been used to just Milo's donkey - walking. But when I got there, the WingCo came out - he was called Wing Commander Mitchell and his adjutant was Flight Officer Dean. They were both very nice.'

Vera's typing gradually improved and she became a regular at the examination centre. And she had some female company - Deanna Happel.

'We were treated very well and were always picked up from Twyford station by this camouflaged car. The porter must have wondered what on earth was going on, particularly when more and more people needed to go to the house and I ended up sitting on the WingCo's knee!'

As the only two women at the house, Deanna and Vera were given their own bathroom, a real luxury for a woman who lived in a cottage with basic washing facilities.

'I used to take my bits and pieces with me and wash them there. You know, stockings and knickers and underwear. There was hot water at the house and I could hang them all up to dry, so it was very useful.'

Because their bathroom was for the use of the two women only and all men were strictly forbidden to enter it, Vera was confident that her drying undergarments would remain hidden from male eyes.

'We used to go to the pub at lunchtime and have a few drinks. I came back one day and went to do my washing but there was somebody in the toilet part of the bathroom. Well, it was obviously a man, and he wasn't supposed to be in there, so I decided to teach him a lesson. I did my washing - leisurely - and hung it all up, then I ran a bath and got into it and stayed in for ages, singing very loudly as I wallowed. The poor chap had to stay in the toilet for the whole time as he could not risk being discovered somewhere that was strictly out of bounds!'

Vera was then transferred to the Air Ministry in London where she worked on medical boards for the man who became a pioneer in the world of plastic surgery.

'Sir Archibald McIndoe did a lot of work with skin grafts - particularly facial - where pilots had been badly burned. He did a lot of work at the East Grinstead burns unit, but I worked for him in London. He was a lovely man. Sir Edward Lutyens was in the next office along the corridor. He was very charming, too.'

Vera continued to keep records and type reports at the Air Ministry, working closely with Sir Archibald. She was also often present at the medical boards.

'They were really interesting. These men had been badly burned and he really helped them. He once did over seventy operations on one man's face to rebuild it.'

As an Air Ministry worker, she was also required to help in the defence of the building during raids. She joined the Air Ministry Fire Service and took her turn on fire watching duties.

'We had our tin hats and we had to do two hour stints. We had iron beds where we had to sleep until it was our turn, and then we'd have to go up the ladder and onto the roof. I used to dread being called up there.'

As the bombs and incendiaries dropped, the draught they created was terrifying.

'Well, it was all very haphazard. The walls around the edge of the roof were very low and if one had gone off, we'd have just been blown straight off. We were supposed to knock any off the building and report where they were all falling. We didn't have any protection at all - except our tin hats of course.'

Although it was haphazard, fire watching was an important part of civil duty during the war years. Fire watchers were given specific training for their role.

'We had to crawl through smoke across the gravel and we wore boiler suits when we did fire watching stuff. The men from St Clements Press next door used to whistle at us while we were doing this - bottoms in the air, crawling across the gravel. Smoke rises - so we had to crawl under it. That's what we had to do.'

Then there was the actual fire fighting and working the hoses. To help manoeuvre them quickly to where they were needed, the Air Ministry Fire Service had its own transport.

'We had this little cart that we used to hitch down Kingsway. We had these heavy canvas hoses with half-inch nozzles. Well, you had to lay across them to direct them where you wanted them to go. It was hard work man-handlding them. They had a life of their own.'

Vera now lives near Hampton Court.

CHAPTER THIRTY NINE

Pauline Smith - War Widow

Pauline Smith and her parents had lived on the Surrey/London border for many years. Unlike today, life then was far more settled. It was not unusual to marry within a close community; neighbours, school friends or acquaintances. Pauline joined this tradition when she married a boy she had known since her schooldays, the brother of her best friend Kathleen.

'Kathleen and I went to Merton Central School together and her brother, Eric, went to Tiffin School near Kingston. I'd been going out with him on and off for several years by the time we got married.'

At five years older than the eighteen year old Pauline, he was already in the Navy before war started and had ambitions to become an officer.

'He'd have been a captain. He came from a naval family. His father had been in the Navy and it's just what they did. It was in his blood'.

At the time of their wedding, Eric was a Petty Officer. He wore his best uniform for the service held at Raynes Park Church on 1st February 1941. Pauline, who had refused her mother's request for her to get married in white, was resplendent in a brown fur jacket and cape.

After the wedding, they had just three days together before Eric had to rejoin his ship.

As a married woman, Pauline was not required for specific war work and she continued in her job as a shorthand typist in London. With her husband away, she had no need to move out of her family home.

It was not unusual for couples to be separated without any contact. Wives frequently had little idea of where their men were once they had been posted.

In May 1941, Pauline received news of her husband from an unexpected source.

'I heard it on the wireless. HMS Kashmir and HMS Kelly had both been sunk off the coast of Crete on May 23rd 1941. I knew that Eric was on the Kashmir - that was his ship and that was how I heard the news - on the wireless, just like that'.

They had been married for just over six weeks.

'I'd gone to work and Dad came up to London with the telegram. It said that Eric was missing but that there was a possibility that he had survived and got ashore safely. That was all it said, nothing else.'

Telegrams were deliberately and necessarily brief during wartime. Given the circumstances, Pauline could only wait. Then she heard that there had been survivors from both HMS Kashmir and HMS Kelly. Lord Mountbatten had been rescued from the wreck of the Kelly but no other names had been released.

'I always hated Louis Mountbatten. Not hated him really but he'd survived and my husband was missing. I just wanted to know. But there was no news. It was very difficult.'

Some months later she received a letter from the Captain of HMS Kashmir.

'He said that many men had got out of the ship and that some had definitely made it ashore, where they were helped by locals. But he also said that Eric had been in the part of the ship where the bomb had hit, so nobody could say for sure but it meant that there was little hope that he had got out. After I got that letter, I knew. I just felt that he was dead.'

Pauline spent four years wondering and waiting for further news.

As a married woman with a husband officially missing, Pauline faced a difficult situation. Although legally married, she was socially single, yet public opinion prevented her from repairing her life. If she started another relationship, what would happen if Eric suddenly appeared? And how would his family react, especially as her best friend was also her sister-in-law? But unless she tried to deal with her loss, how could she hope to move her life forward?

Pauline remained outside any defined social group with which she could have identified. Had she been single, she could have joined the Forces or the Land Army. Such work would have offered her a sense of camaraderie and given her support during a difficult and traumatic time.

Without confirmation of Eric's death, Pauline received no pension or allowance until after the war had finished. During those years she had had to fend for herself, financially, emotionally and socially.

Pauline rebuilt her life, but still reflects on what might have been.

'I often wonder what would have happened and what my life would have been like had Eric lived. I wasn't unusual - lots of women lost their husbands, but I've often thought about it. It seems such a long time ago now and it's like a dream, but when I remember him, I still see him as he was in those three days that we were together. I never saw him as an old man or a middle-aged man, just as the young man I married.'

Pauline still lives on the Surrey/London border.

CHAPTER FORTY

Lily Wray - Mother

While many women were thoroughly immersed in war work, others continued in their peacetime role, adapting it as necessary.

Lily was living in the North East, at Billingham, County Durham with her husband and daughter when the war started.

'My husband joined the Home Guard and when the alert went, he'd just have to dash off and leave us. It didn't matter what we were doing, he'd just down everything and go. Up in Billingham, we had the ICI factory and they used to bomb that, the Germans. We also had the buzz bombs, too. It was frightening for the children as well as for the adults. But you had to pretend everything was OK just for their sakes.'

Few places in Britain escaped air raids. Many spent countless nights in the shelters, which were rarely comfortable.

Most had been built with whatever people could find to help strengthen the structure and make it warmer. It was not uncommon to find a motley collection of items had been used. Lily's shelter near the Tees Estuary, was better equipped and perhaps slightly more unusual than most.

'The cinema across the road had shut down and so we bought some seats off them. We paid a shilling a seat and put them down the shelter, so it was quite nice really - cold, but nice. Later when the bombing got worse and we had more people in there, we used hammocks. We strung them up across the shelter.'

Whether they worked in paid employment or worked in the home, it was women like Lily who kept life as steady as possible for their children and other people around them. If they all carried on as normally as possible, or as circumstances allowed then, perhaps, the relative calm of pre-war life would continue - for just that little bit longer.

After the war Lily moved south and became courturier to Odette Churchill, the Special Operations Executive agent.

'She was always very elegant. A very nice woman. I only found out who she was years later.'

Lily now lives in Surrey.